Guardianstyle

Guardianstyle

David Marsh

guardianbooks

First published in 2007 by
Guardian Books, 119 Farringdon Road, London EC1R 3ER
www.guardian.co.uk

Guardian Books is an imprint of Guardian News and Media Ltd
Copyright © The Guardian 2007

A CIP record for this book is available from the British Library

ISBN: 978-0-85265-086-8

Cover design: Two Associates
Text design: www.carrstudio.co.uk

Printed and bound in Great Britain by MPG Books, Bodmin,
Cornwall.

Contents

Acknowledgments

Very special thanks to Amelia Hodsdon, a superb subeditor and proofreader who has devoted a lot of time and attention to these pages.

Thanks also to Richard Alcock, Andy Bodle, Helen Brooks, Kirsten Broomhall (who wrote the section on web style), Charlotte Dewar, Chris Hall, and Anna Bawden (for sorting out beeper and bleeper, and much more).

This book would not be possible without the contributions of Guardian and Guardian Unlimited readers, with whom my colleagues and I share an invigorating daily dialogue that is reflected in many of the comments and suggestions included here.

A special mention for my former colleague Nikki Marshall, co-author of the previous edition of this book. Her influence and inspiration continue to shine through these pages, even at a distance of 10,000 miles.

Always remembering Patrick.

David Marsh
London, August 2007

The style guide is online at www.guardian.co.uk/styleguide

The email address for your comments, which are very welcome, is style.guide@guardian.co.uk

Introduction

by Ian Mayes

Well, is it bumf or bumph? You can see straightaway why Guardian journalists are required to read this stylebook. It is easily the best one that the paper has had to turn to, and easily the easiest to consult, freely available to all at the click of a mouse. This is the second edition and it is much larger than the first, something that is not attributable to any loss of concentration or falling away of standards: since the book appeared, three years ago, the Guardian has twice won the Plain English Campaign's award for the best national newspaper, earning praise for the clarity of its language and, according to the citation, continuing to set the standard for others. No, the book has been extended, and in a few cases corrected, through the keen attentions not only of Guardian journalists but, much more than in the past, of readers from all over the world. They have leaped at the opportunity to participate. The daily corrections column is a standing invitation to do just that, and the inclusion of comments from readers throughout this new edition shows that the invitation is a genuine one and that the response is more than welcome. We are in this together.

In fact, to say that journalists are "required" to read the stylebook may suggest that it could be considered a bit of a chore. Hardly. For a great many of us, probably including you reading this now, it is exciting and necessary stuff, moving enough to have had us reaching for a pen or hastening to our keyboard, perhaps in an initial lather. It shows that we all care not just about what is said but the way in which it is said. Of course, in print or online a newspaper is a newspaper, a machine whose tendency to err is a constant challenge to its operators (I don't wish to make excuses). Perfection in the circumstances is not possible. Most of us for most of the time want to be reasonable. People can sometimes become very unreasonable. Vasily Grossman, in Life and Fate, his account of life in the gulag (translated by Robert Chandler), records this meeting with a released prisoner: "He had been a proofreader on a newspaper and had spent seven years in the camps for missing a misprint in a leading article – the typesetter had got one letter wrong in Stalin's name." Well, of course, names are important.

Today the proofreader in that sense no longer exists. Nowadays journalists have only themselves to blame for mistakes that escape all the checks. They are the checkers. The stylebook – you must concede at least this – is evidence of the huge effort the Guardian makes to contain the "shimmer of errors" that Vladimir Nabokov, or rather Humbert Humbert, suggested was a characteristic of newspapers.

It can be a subtle business. Many entries emphasise distinctions between words often misused or confused: doner, kebab; donor, gives money (did someone resist the temptation to say "donor, kidney"?); hyperthermia, hot; hypothermia, cold; disinterested, free from bias or objective; uninterested, not taking an interest; hangar for aircraft, hanger for clothes. Grammar is defined, while saving us all the shame of pointing out that it occasionally appears as grammer.

Some institutional idiocies are addressed. For example, the entry for "total'" wisely advises: "avoid starting court stories with variations on the formula 'three men were jailed for a total of 19 years', a statistic that contains no meaningful information ... " Bertolt Brecht struggled to come close to sense with this kind of addition when he wrote of two bankers in Threepenny Novel: "Together they were more than 150 years old, and when one had to deal with them one had to deal with one and a half centuries" (translated by Desmond Vesey). In news stories it rarely adds up to add up.

The "apostrofly" – the rogue insect that I can claim to have discovered – continues to alight in unlikely spots, as one of the readers quoted here noticed: "I've seen some choice grocer's apostrophes in the past, but I think 'The Orkney's' in today's Guardian takes the biscuit." A fairly long entry on the apostrophe attempts to put it in its (no apostrophe) place: we shall keep trying.

This edition includes an essay, a mini-workshop, on headline writing by the editor of the stylebook, David Marsh, who demonstrates what a tricky business it can be — "Book lack in Ongar", about a crisis in the Essex library service, is still one of my favourites. He cautions subeditors about punning to tedium, where they nearly went with headlines in the 1980s. There is also a timely and informative essay on web style, by the chief news subeditor of Guardian Unlimited, Kirsten Broomhall. She explains how style can vary — how it is varied — to meet the developing requirements of what is already a multimedia website without departing from the values common to the whole Guardian. Both of these essays expose the inner thinkings and workings in a way that now comes more or less naturally to the Guardian.

The more important entries, on terminology to do with race, disability, terrorism and terrorists, among other matters, are worthy of serious study and afford insights into, what shall I call it, the Guardian mind. Generally, it is a book for browsing, but perhaps too controversial a book for bedtime. A great many of the entries seek to resolve clamorous disputes, the noise of which has not in all cases completely died away. The question of the Guardian's use of capitals and lower case, for example, is not the call to arms it once was, even if it still causes occasional skirmishes. The book, and this is a case in point, is all about persuasion and persistence, and sometimes compromise. It invites a response from you. Many of the entries are the result of responses from you. Thank you for that.

By the way, it is bumf, but then we all knew that, didn't we?

Ian Mayes is the former readers' editor and an associate editor of the Guardian. He is writing the history of the Guardian since the 1980s

Glossary

adjectives modify nouns, as in "she had a quick drink"

adverbs modify verbs, as in "she drank quickly"

audio slideshow an automated online photo gallery with running commentary

Berliner (also **midi**) newspaper format, narrower and shorter than a broadsheet, taller and wider than a tabloid; the Guardian switched to Berliner format on September 12 2005

blog a collection of online articles, and the action of publishing an article to the blog by a **blogger**

blurb copy pointing to an article elsewhere in the newspaper or one of its other publications

cap up start the word with a capital letter

captions text describing a photograph or image

City editor journalist in charge of the business section

compositor a person who set type for printing (before newspaper pages were created on computer programs)

copy the main body text of an article

copy editor US version of a subeditor, also someone who copy-edits books

desk editors journalists who plan their section's coverage and assign stories to reporters

display quotes extracts from an article reproduced in a larger type, set into the body of the text

editor is to newspaper or website as captain is to ship

Fleet Street nickname for Britain's national newspapers (their former home)

full out write in full rather than abbreviate

furniture the explanatory text around the main copy (headline, standfirst, caption etc)

G2 the Guardian's daily features section

G3s the Guardian's weekly features sections, covering specialised areas such as education

GU the Guardian Unlimited website

headline, head text in large bold type trumpeting an article

homepage the main page of a website, such as the Guardian Unlimited network

italicise use italics, *like this*

keywords used when searching for a specific item on the web: for example, putting the keywords "guardian" and "style guide" into a search engine would help a user find the Guardian style guide online

lc lower case

leader article on comment pages expressing a newspaper's opinion, also known as **leader comment** or **leading article**

line break where a line of copy ends

link (noun) takes the reader to a relevant reference elsewhere on the GU site or the wider internet

link (verb) to insert a relevant reference into an article or blog

podcast a digital broadcast that can be listened to on a personal computer, or downloaded on to portable media players such as an iPod

post (also **blogpost**) single article on a blog, and the action of publishing an article to the blog

reporters gather news and write articles

roman ordinary lettering, not **bold** or *italicised*

running text the main body copy of an article

spike reject a story (named after the metal spike on which pages of unwanted copy were impaled)

sources people willing to talk to journalists

spin usually refers to public relations strategies used by a government to cast a flattering light on its activities

standfirsts a sub-heading or secondary headline, in smaller text and often running across a page and over a photograph

story not a work of fiction, but a news article or feature

subeditor, sub journalist who lays out (designs) pages, edits, checks and cuts copy, and writes headlines, captions and standfirsts

tabloid refers to long-standing red-tops such as the Sun and the Daily Mirror, rather than the new breed of shrunken broadsheets

tabloidese punning, sensational style beloved of tabloid journalists

thin (non-breaking) space inserted by subeditors between words that should not straddle a line break, eg leg-end

trailblock a collection of relevant links at the bottom of an online article

transitive verbs take an object, as in "she stroked the cat"; **intransitive verbs** do not take an object, as in "his dog died"

transliteration writing one language in the alphabet of another

uc UPPER CASE

wires breaking stories and features written by staff at news agencies such as Reuters and sent to subscribers

Aa

"He's supposed to have a particularly
high-class style: 'Feather-footed through
the plashy fen passes the questing vole' …
would that be it?

"Yes," said the Managing Editor. "That
must be good style. At least it doesn't
sound like anything else to me."

Evelyn Waugh, Scoop

a or **an**? use an before a silent H: an hour, an heir, an honourable man, an honest woman; a hero, a hotel, a historian (but don't change a direct quote if the speaker says, for example, "an historic"). With abbreviations, be guided by pronunciation: eg an LSE student

A* (GCSE) not A-star

A&E accident and emergency

abattoir

abbeys are, like cathedrals, capped up: Westminster Abbey, Canterbury Cathedral, etc

abbreviations and acronyms

Do not use full points in abbreviations, or spaces between initials: US, mph, eg, 4am, lbw, No 10, PJ O'Rourke, WH Smith, etc.

Use all capitals if an abbreviation is pronounced as the individual letters: BBC, VAT, etc; if it is an acronym (pronounced as a word) spell out with initial capital, eg Nasa, Nato, unless it can be considered to have entered the language as an everyday word, such as awol, laser and, more recently, asbo, pin number and sim card.

If an abbreviation or acronym that readers may not immediately recognise is to be used more than once, put it in brackets at first mention, eg Association of Chief Police Officers (Acpo), seasonal affective disorder (Sad). This saves people having to search back through the article to find the original reference.

Use common sense, however: it is not necessary to spell out well-known ones, such as EU, UN, CIA, FBI, CD, Nasa, etc.

Cap up single letters in such expressions as A-list, F-word, "the word assassin contains four Ss", etc *see contractions*

aborigines, aboriginal lc when referring to indigenous populations

Aborigines, Aboriginal uc when referring to native Australians

abscess

absorb but **absorption**

abysmal

abyss

a cappella

Acas the Advisory, Conciliation and Arbitration Service at first mention, thereafter just Acas

accents

Use on French, German, Spanish and Irish Gaelic words (but not anglicised French words such as cafe, apart from exposé, pâté, résumé, roué); people's names, in whatever language, should also be given appropriate accents

Accenture formerly Andersen Consulting

access has been known as **contact** since the 1989 Children Act *see custody*

accommodate, accommodation

accordion

achilles heel, achilles tendon

acknowledgment not acknowledgement

Aa

acres use hectares, with acres in brackets, rounded up: eg the field measured 25 hectares (62 acres); you multiply hectares by 2.47 to convert to acres, or acres by 0.4 to convert to hectares

acronyms *see abbreviations and acronyms*

act uc when using full name, eg Criminal Justice Act 1998, Official Secrets Act; but lc on second reference, eg "the act", and when speaking in more general terms, eg "we need a radical freedom of information act"; bills remain lc until passed into law

acting always lc: acting prime minister, acting committee chair, etc

actor for both male and female actors; do not use actress except when in name of award, eg Oscar for best actress; one 27-year-old actor contacted the Guardian to say "actress" has acquired a faintly pejorative tinge and she wants people to call her actor (except for her agent, who should call her often).
As always, use common sense: a piece about the late film director Carlo Ponti was changed to say that in his early career he was "already a man with a good eye for pretty actors" ... As the readers' editor pointed out in the subsequent clarification: "This was one of those occasions when the word 'actresses' might have been used"

AD, BC AD goes before the date (AD64), BC goes after (300BC); both go after the century, eg second century AD, fourth century BC

adaptation not adaption

adapter someone who adapts; **adaptor** plug

addendum plural **addendums**

addresses 119 Farringdon Road, London EC1R 3ER

Adidas initial cap

administration the Clinton administration, etc

admissible, inadmissible not -able

admit take care; as the great Washington Post editor Ben Bradlee put it: "No story is fair if reporters hide their biases and emotions behind such subtly pejorative words as refused, despite, admit and massive"

adoption

Mention that children are adopted only when relevant to the story: a reader points out that "explicitly calling attention to adoptions in this way suggests that adoption is not as good, and not as real a relationship, as having a child normally".

So say biological father, biological family rather than "real father", "real family", etc

Adrenalin TM; a brand of adrenaline

adrenaline hormone that increases heart rate and blood pressure, extracted from animals or synthesised for medical uses

adverbs

Do not use hyphens after adverbs ending in -ly, eg a hotly disputed penalty, a constantly evolving newspaper, genetically modified food, etc; but hyphens are needed with short and common adverbs, eg ever-forgiving family, ill-prepared report, much-loved character, well-founded suspicion

adviser not advisor

advocate member of the Scottish bar (not a barrister)

aeroplane use **airplane**

affect/effect exhortations in the style guide had no effect (noun) on the number of mistakes; the level of mistakes was not affected (verb) by exhortations in the style guide; we hope to effect (verb) a change in this

affidavit a written declaration made on oath, so "sworn affidavit" is tautologous

affinity with or between, not to or for

Afghans people; **Afghanis** currency of Afghanistan

aficionado plural **aficionados**

African-Caribbean not Afro-Caribbean

Afrikaans language; **Afrikaner** person

afterlife, aftermath

ageing

ages Gordon Brown, 56 (not "aged 56"); little Johnny, four; the woman was in her 20s (but twentysomething, thirtysomething, etc)

aggravate to make worse, not to annoy

aggro despite the once-popular terrace chant "A, G, A-G-R, A-G-R-O: agro!"

AGM not agm

ahead of avoid, use before or in advance of

aide-de-camp plural **aides-de-camp** (aide is a noun)

aide-memoire plural **aide-memoires** (aide is a verb)

Aids acquired immune deficiency syndrome, but normally no need to spell out.

Don't use such terms as "Aids victims" or someone "suffering from Aids", language that in the words of one reader is "crass, inaccurate and reinforces stigma", implying helplessness and inviting pity; "people with Aids" (or "living with Aids") is preferable

airbase, aircraft, aircrew, airdrop, airlift, airmail, airplane, airstrip, airtime

aircraft carrier no hyphen

air fares, air force, air raid, air show, air strike .

Air Force One US president's jet

air hostess *see cabin attendant*

airports Heathrow, Gatwick, Stansted (normally no need to say airport); Liverpool John Lennon airport, Schiphol airport, etc

air vice-marshal

AKA also known as

akimbo *see arms akimbo*

al- (note lc and hyphen) before an Arabic name means "the" so try to avoid writing "the al- ... " where possible *see Arabic names*

al-Aqsa Martyrs Brigade

al-Assad, Bashar Syrian politician

Alastair or **Alistair**?

Alastair Campbell
Alastair Cook (Essex and England cricketer)
Alastair Hetherington

Alistair Cooke (former BBC and Guardian journalist)
Alistair Darling
Alistair Maclean
Alistair McGowan

Aleister Crowley

Albright, Madeleine former US secretary of state

Alcott, Louisa May (1832-88) American author of Little Women

A-levels

Al Fayed, Mohamed owner of Harrods (Fayed after first mention; Mr Fayed if honorific is needed); the son who died in Paris in 1997 was Dodi Fayed

Alfonsín, Raúl former Argentinian president

alfresco

algae plural of **alga**; algal bloom not algae bloom

Ali, Muhammad

alibi being somewhere else; not synonymous with excuse

alice band as worn by Alice in Lewis Carroll's Through the Looking-Glass (1871) and more recently David Beckham

A-list etc, but to refer to "C-list celebrities" and its variations has become tedious. An edition of G2 referred to "D-list celebrities" and, less than hilariously, in a separate piece about the same reality TV show, "Z-list celebrities"

Congratulations on the stylebook. I was very disappointed that you have given no guidance on ass/arse. I raised this matter with the Guardian nearly 50 years ago. My letter was published but evidently no heed was paid to it. I really think this is a matter on which our greatest newspaper should have made an ex cathedra announcement years ago.

Tony Brooks,
Hastings

al-Jazeera

Allah

Arabic for "the God". Both words refer to the same concept: there is no major difference between God in the Old Testament and Allah in Islam. Therefore it makes sense to talk about "God" in an Islamic context and to use "Allah" in quotations or for literary effect

Allahu Akbar "God is greatest"

all comers

Allende, Isabel Chilean author, niece of Salvador

Allende, Salvador Chilean president, overthrown and killed in 1973

allies second world war allies, etc

all mouth and trousers not "all mouth and no trousers"

allot, allotted

all right is right; alright is not all right (but note the Who song, much loved by generations of headline writers, was The Kids Are Alright)

All Souls College Oxford, no apostrophe

al-Majid, General Ali Hassan member of Saddam Hussein's revolutionary command council, nicknamed Chemical Ali for his atrocities against Iraq's Kurds and sentenced to death in 2007 (Majid on second reference)

al-Maliki, Nouri (not Nuri) became prime minister of Iraq in 2006

Almo arm's-length management organisation

Almodóvar, Pedro Spanish film-maker

alone often redundant

al-Qaida Osama bin Laden's organisation; it means "the base"

alsatian dog; **Alsatian** person from Alsace

also often redundant

AltaVista

alter ego we have been known to spell it "altar ego" (to be used only as a headline on a story about an arrogant bishop)

alternative normally a choice between two courses of action; if there are more than two, option or choice may be preferred; beware the trend to use "alternate" instead of alternative: in a piece about French politics we wrote "in this juddering alternate reality … "

alumnus plural **alumni**

Alzheimer's disease

AM (assembly member) member of the Welsh assembly, eg Rhodri Morgan AM

Amazon normally no need for com or co.uk

ambassador lc, eg the British ambassador to Washington; "the ambassador's receptions are noted in society for their host's exquisite taste"

ambience not ambiance

America, Americans although like most people we use these to mean the United States and its citizens, we should remember that America includes all of North and South America

American Civil Liberties Union not American Civil Rights Union

American English

In general, use British English spellings: secretary of defence, Labour Day, World Trade Centre, etc; exceptions are placenames such as Ann Arbor, Pearl Harbor

American universities

Take care: "University of X" is not the same as "X University"; most states have two large public universities, eg University of Kentucky and Kentucky State University, University of Illinois and Illinois State University, etc

Do not call Johns Hopkins University "John Hopkins" or Stanford University "Stamford"

America's Cup

Amhrán na bhFiann Irish national anthem

Amicus trade union formed by a merger between the AEEU and MSF, now part of Unite after a further merger with the TGWU

amid not amidst

amok not amuck

among not amongst

among or between?

Contrary to popular myth, between is not limited to two parties. It is appropriate when the relationship is essentially reciprocal: fighting between the many peoples of Yugoslavia, treaties between European countries. Among belongs to distributive relationships: shared among, etc

ampersand use in company names when the company does: Marks & Spencer, P&O

anaesthetic

analysis plural **analyses**

ancestors precede descendants; we frequently manage to get them the wrong way round

Andalucía

Anderson shelter not Andersen

anglicise, anglophile, anglophone

annex verb; **annexe** noun

anonymous quotes see Appendix 2: the editor's guidelines on the identification of sources

Ansaphone TM; use **answering machine** or **answerphone**

antenna (insect) plural **antennae**; (radio) plural **antennas**

anti-ballistic missile treaty

antichrist

anticipate take action in expectation of; not synonymous with expect

anticlimax

antidepressants

antihero

antipodean, antipodes

antisemitic, antisemitism

antisocial

anti-war

any more two words

apex plural apexes

apostrofly "an insect that lands at random on the printed page, depositing an apostrophe wherever it lands", according to the Guardian's former readers' editor

I am reading your stylebook from cover to cover and loving it. May I suggest an update at the entry "alice band"? Anyone who has seen Beckham's hair recently will know, with the present winter weather, that he's more in need of a wig.

Jacqueline Karp, Vaux-sur-Mer, France

apostrophes

These indicate a missing letter or letters (can't, we'd) or a possessive (David's book).

Some shops use an apostrophe, wrongly, to indicate a plural ("pea's"), but will generally omit the apostrophe when one is actually required ("new seasons asparagus"), a phenomenon sometimes referred to as the greengrocer's (or grocer's) apostrophe. Try to avoid this.

Contractions can affect the tone of a piece and make it appear informal and even inelegant: "what's more" may work in a lighthearted column but "what is more" may be more appropriate for a leading article.

The possessive in words and names ending in S normally takes an apostrophe followed by a second S (Jones's, James's), but be guided by pronunciation and use the plural apostrophe where it helps: Mephistopheles', Waters', Hedges' rather than Mephistopheles's, Waters's, Hedges's.

Plural nouns that do not end in S take an apostrophe and S in the possessive: children's games, old folk's home, people's republic, etc.

Phrases such as butcher's knife, collector's item, cow's milk, goat's cheese, pig's blood, hangman's noose, writer's cramp, etc are treated as singular.

Use apostrophes in phrases such as two days' time, 12 years' imprisonment and six weeks' holiday, where the time period (two days) modifies a noun (time), but not in nine months pregnant or three weeks old, where the time period is adverbial (modifying an adjective such as pregnant or old) – if in doubt, test with a singular such as one day's time, one month pregnant.

Finally, if anyone tries to tell you that apostrophes don't matter and we'd be better off without them, consider these four phrases, each of which means something different:

my sister's friend's investments
my sisters' friends' investments
my sisters' friend's investments
my sister's friends' investments

appal, appalling

apparatchik

appendix plural **appendices**

Apple Computer not Computers; former name of Apple

apples lc: cox's orange pippin, golden delicious, granny smith, etc

appraise to evaluate

apprise to inform

aquarium plural **aquariums**

Arab

Both a noun and an adjective, and the preferred adjective when referring to Arab things in general, eg Arab history, Arab traditions. Arabic usually refers to the language and literature: "the Arabic press" means newspapers written in Arabic, while "the Arab press" would include newspapers produced by Arabs in other languages.

There is no simple definition of an Arab. At an international level, the 22 members of the Arab League can safely be described as Arab countries: Algeria, Bahrain, Comoros, Djibouti, Egypt, Iraq, Jordan, Kuwait, Lebanon, Libya, Mauritania, Morocco, Oman, Palestine, Qatar, Saudi Arabia, Somalia, Sudan, Syria, Tunisia, United Arab Emirates, and Yemen. At a human level, there are substantial groups within those countries – the Berbers of north Africa and the Kurds, for example – who do not regard themselves as Arabs

Arabic names

Though Arabic has only three vowels – a, i and u – it has several consonants that have no equivalent in the Roman alphabet. For instance, there are two kinds of s, d and t. There are also two glottal sounds. This means there are at least 32 ways of writing the Libyan leader Muammar Gadafy's name in English, and a reasonable argument can be made for adopting almost any of them. With no standard approach to transliteration agreed by the western media, we must try to balance consistency, comprehensibility and familiarity – which often puts a strain on all three.

Typically, Arabs have at least three names. In some cases the first or second name may be the one that is most used, and this does not imply familiarity. Often Arabs also have familiar names that have no connection with the names on their identity cards: a man might become known after the birth of his first son as "Abu Ahmad", and a woman as "Umm Ahmad", the father or mother of Ahmad (eg the Palestinian leader Ahmed Qureia is commonly known as Abu Ala).

Where a particular spelling has become widely accepted through usage we should retain it. Where an individual with links to the west has clearly adopted a particular spelling of his or her own name, we should respect that. For breaking news and stories using names for which the Guardian has no established style, we take the lead given by Reuters wire copy.

Note also that names in some parts of the Arab world have become gallicised, while others have become anglicised, eg the leading Egyptian film director Youssef Chahine uses a French spelling instead of the English transliteration, Shaheen.

Some guidelines (for use particularly where there is no established transliteration):

al-

Means "the". In names it is not capitalised, eg Ahmad al-Saqqaf, and can be dropped after the first mention (Saqqaf). For placenames the Guardian drops it altogether. Sometimes it appears as as- or ash- or ad- or ul-: these should be ignored and can be safely rewritten as al-. But some Arabs, including Syrians and Egyptians, prefer to use el- in place of al-. Exceptions: by convention, **Allah** (al-Lah, literally "the

God") is written as one word and capitalised; and in Saudi royal names, **Al Saud** is correct (in this case, "al" is actually "aal" and does not mean "the").

abdul, abu and bin

These are not self-contained names, but are connected to the name that follows:

abdul means "slave of ... " and so cannot correctly be used on its own. There are standard combinations, "slave of the merciful one", "slave of the generous one", etc, which all indicate that the person is a servant of God. In transliteration, "abd" (slave) is lower case, eg Ahmad abd al-Rahman al-Saqqaf, except when used at the start of a name.

abu (father of) and **bin** (son of) are similar. When they appear in the middle of a name they should be lower case and are used in combination with the following part of the name: Faisal abu Ahmad al-Saqqaf, Faisal bin Ahmad al-Saqqaf.

Despite the above, some people are actually known as "Abdul". This is more common among non-Arab Muslims. And some Arabs run "abd" or "abu" into the following word, eg the writer Abdelrahman Munif.

Muhammad

Our style for the prophet's name and for most Muhammads living in Arab countries, though where someone's preferred spelling is known we respect it, eg Mohamed Al Fayed, Mohamed ElBaradei. The spelling Mohammed (or variants) is considered archaic by most British Muslims, and disrespectful by many of them.

Muhandis/Mohandes, Qadi

Be wary of names where the first word is Muhandis or Qadi: these are honorary titles, meaning engineer and judge respectively

Arafat, Yasser

Aran Island is off Co Donegal and the **Aran Islands** off Co Galway in western Ireland; the **Isle of Arran** is the largest island in the Firth of Clyde in Scotland. **Aran sweaters**, whether Irish or Scottish, are lower case with an initial cap A

archbishops the Archbishop of Canterbury, the Right Rev Rowan Williams, at first mention, thereafter Williams or the archbishop; the Archbishop of Westminster, Cardinal Cormac Murphy-O'Connor, on first mention, subsequently Murphy-O'Connor or the archbishop

archdeacon the Ven Paul Olive, Archdeacon of Farringdon, at first mention; then just Olive, or the archdeacon

archery arrows are shot, rather than fired; and if they hit the centre of the target, it is a gold rather than a bullseye

archipelago plural **archipelagos**

arch-rival

Ardoyne (Belfast), not "the Ardoyne"

Argentine noun and adjective; not Argentinian

arguably unarguably one of the most overused words in the language

Armageddon

armed forces, armed services

army, the, the **British army, the navy**, but **Royal Navy, Royal Air Force** or **RAF**

arms akimbo hands on hips, elbows out; it is surprising how often the phrase "legs akimbo" turns up in the paper, "suggesting that such a posture exists, but lacks a word to define it", as David McKie wrote

around about or approximately are better, eg "about £1m" or "approximately 2,000 people"

around or **round**? We were driving around aimlessly all weekend; it nearly drove me round the bend

arranged marriages are a traditional and perfectly acceptable form of wedlock across southern Asia and within the Asian community in Britain; they should not be confused with **forced marriages**, which are arranged without the consent of one or both partners, and have been widely criticised

arse British English; **ass** American English

art movements lc, **art deco, art nouveau, cubism, dadaism, expressionism, gothic, impressionism, pop art, surrealism**, etc, but **Bauhaus, Modern** (in the sense of Modern British, to distinguish it from "modern art", **pre-Raphaelite, Romantic** (to differentiate between a romantic painting and a Romantic painting)

artefact

artist not artiste (except, possibly, in a historical context)

Arts and Crafts movement

Arts Council England, Arts Council of Wales, Scottish Arts Council

as or **since**? "as" is causal: I cannot check the online style guide as the connection is down; "since" is temporal: Luckily, I have had the stylebook on my desk since it was published

asbo

ascendancy, ascendant

Ash Action on Smoking and Health

Ashura a day of voluntary fasting for Muslims; Shia Muslims also commemorate the martyrdom of Hussein, a grandson of the prophet, so for them it is not a festival but a day of mourning

Asperger's syndrome

aspirin

assassin, assassination the murder of prominent political figures rather than, say, celebrities

Association of Chief Police Officers is on second mention **Acpo**

astrologer not astrologist

astronomer royal

Asunción capital of Paraguay

asylum seeker

Someone seeking refugee status or humanitarian protection; there is no such thing as an "illegal asylum seeker", a term the Press Complaints Commission ruled in breach of its code of practice.

Refugees are people who have fled their home countries in fear for their lives, and may have been granted asylum under the 1951 refugee convention or qualify for humanitarian protection or discretionary leave, or have been granted exceptional leave to remain in Britain.

An asylum seeker can become an illegal immigrant only if he or she remains in Britain after having failed to respond to a removal notice

ATCU Associated Train Crew Union; not to be confused with ACTU, the Australian Council of Trade Unions

athletics write **1500m** but **5,000m** (the former is the "fifteen hundred" not "one thousand five hundred" metres)

Atlantic Ocean or just the Atlantic

attache no accent

attention deficit hyperactivity disorder ADHD after first mention

Attlee, Clement (1883-1967) Labour prime minister 1945-51, often misspelt as Atlee

attorney general lc, no hyphen

auger used to make holes; **augur** predict or presage

Aum Shinrikyo means Supreme Truth sect, but note that the "aum" means sect, so to talk about the "Aum sect" or "Aum cult" is tautologous

Auntie not Aunty if you must refer to the BBC in this way

au pair

Australasia use **Oceania**

Australian Labor party not Labour

autism neurological disorder, to be used only when referring to the condition, not as a term of abuse, or in producing such witticisms as "mindless moral autism" and "Star Wars is a form of male autism", both of which have appeared in the paper

autistic someone with autism, not someone with poor social skills

Autocue TM; **teleprompter** is a generic alternative

autumn

avant garde no hyphen

average, mean and median

Although we loosely refer to the "average" in many contexts (eg pay), there are two useful averages worth distinguishing.

What is commonly known as the average is the **mean**: everyone's wages are added up and divided by the number of wage earners. The **median** is described as "the value below which 50% of employees fall", ie it is the wage earned by the middle person when everyone's wages are lined up from smallest to largest. (For even numbers there are two middle people, but you calculate the mean average of their two wages.)

The median is often a more useful guide than the mean, which can be distorted by figures at one extreme or the other

awards, prizes, medals are generally lc, eg Guardian first book award, Nobel peace prize, Fields medal (exceptions: the Academy Awards, Victoria Cross); note that categories are lc, eg "he took the best actor Oscar at the awards"

awol stands for "absent without leave" but, having been around since at least the 1920s, has established itself as a word in its own right

awopbopaloobop alopbamboom

axing not axeing, but cutting jobs is less cliched than axing them

axis plural **axes**

Ayers Rock now known as **Uluru**

Azerbaijan noun; **Azerbaijani** adjective; note that there are ethnic Azeris living in, for example, Armenia

Aznar, José María former prime minister of Spain

Bb

"Do not put statements in the negative form. And don't start sentences with a conjunction. If you reread your work, you will find on rereading that a great deal of repetition can be avoided by rereading and editing. Never use a long word when a diminutive one will do. Unqualified superlatives are the worst of all. De-accession euphemisms. If any word is improper at the end of a sentence, a linking verb is. Avoid trendy locutions that sound flaky. Last, but not least, avoid cliches like the plague."

William Safire

b bit or binary digit; **B** byte, usually made up of 8 bits *see byte*

BAA formerly the British Airports Authority

Ba'ath

Babybel cheese

baby Bells US regional telephone companies formed after the breakup of AT&T in 1984

baby boomer

Babygro TM; a generic alternative is **babygrow**

babysitter

baccalaureate

Bacharach, Burt US songwriter

bachelor now has a slightly old-fashioned ring to it, so probably better to say (if relevant) unmarried man; "confirmed bachelor" should definitely be avoided, as should "bachelor girl" (unless writing about swinging 60s movies)

backbench newspaper or politics; **backbenches, backbenchers**

backstreet, backyard

bacteria plural of **bacterium**, so don't write "the bacteria is"; even more important, don't confuse with viruses

BAE Systems formerly British Aerospace

Bafta British Academy of Film and Television Arts

bagel

Baghdad

Baha'i faith

bail out a prisoner, a company or person in financial difficulty; the noun is **bail-out**; but **bale out** a boat or from an aircraft

bakewell tart

balk obstruct, pull up, stop short; **baulk** area of a snooker table

Ball, Zoë

ballboy, ballgirl but **ball game**

ballot, balloted

Band-Aid TM; say **plaster** or **sticking plaster**

B&B abbreviation for bed and breakfast

band names

lc the: the Beatles, the Black Eyed Peas, the The; but uc equivalents in other languages, eg Les Négresses Vertes, Los Lobos.

Bands that do not take the definite article (though they are often erroneously given it) include Arctic Monkeys, Pet Shop Boys and Ramones; most bands have their own website, or at least webpage, where this can be easily checked.

Bands take a plural verb: Editors are overrated, Iron Butterfly were the loudest band of the 60s, etc.

Try to include diacritical marks if bands use them in their name, no matter how absurd: Maxïmo Park, Mötley Crüe, Motörhead, etc; for a comprehensive list see the excellent "heavy metal umlaut" entry on Wikipedia

Bb

guardian style

Bangalore is now known as **Bengalooru**

bank holiday bank holiday Monday, etc

Ban Ki-moon UN secretary general; Ban on second mention

banknote

Bank of England the Bank on subsequent mentions

Bank of Scotland BoS on second mention

banlieue French for suburbia, not suburb: strictly singular, but a French reader points out that the Petit Robert dictionary listed "les banlieues" among its "nouveaux mots" in 2006; the French for suburb is *faubourg* (literally, "false town")

bar (legal) she was called to the bar; (political) of the House of Commons

barbecue

Barclays Bank

barcode

barmitzvah, batmitzvah

Barnardo's children's charity, formerly Dr Barnardo's; it no longer runs orphanages

barolo wine

Baron Cohen, Sacha the man behind Ali G and Borat

Baron-Cohen, Simon a professor of developmental psychopathology at Cambridge University and cousin of Sacha

barons, baronesses are lords and ladies in the Guardian, even at first mention: Lord Adonis, Lady Scotland, Lady Thatcher, etc; do not use first names with title ("Lady Patricia Scotland")

Barons Court

baroque

barracks the army has barracks, the RAF has airfields

Barroso, José Manuel former prime minister of Portugal who became president of the European commission in 2004

Bart's abbreviation for St Bartholomew's hospital, London

Base jumping extreme sport: the acronym stands for four categories of object from which you can jump, if so inclined: building, antenna, span and earth

basically this word is unnecessary, basically

Basle not Basel

Basque country

bas-relief

bated breath, not baited

Battenberg (not Battenburg) German family name that became Mountbatten; **battenberg cake** lc

Battersea Dogs & Cats Home no apostrophes

battlebus

Bauhaus

BBC1, BBC2, BBC3, BBC4 no spaces

BBC Radio 1, 2, 3, 4, Five Live, 6 Music, BBC7

BC 1000 BC but **AD1066** *see AD*

beau plural **beaux**

Beaver scouts for boys aged six to eight, when they are eligible to become Cub scouts

bebop, hard bop, post-bop

because can be ambiguous: "I didn't go to the party because Mary was there" might mean that Mary's presence dissuaded me from going or that I went for some other reason

Becket, Thomas (1118-70) murdered Archbishop of Canterbury, not Thomas à Becket

bed blocking

bedouin

beef wellington

Beeton, Mrs (Isabella Mary Beeton, 1836-65) author of The Book of Household Management

befitted

begs the question is best avoided as it is almost invariably misused: it means assuming a proposition that, in reality, involves the conclusion. An example would be to say that parallel lines will never meet, because they are parallel, assuming as a fact the thing you are professing to prove. What it does not mean is "raises the question"

Beijing

Belarus adjective **Belarussian**

beleaguered overused, even when we spell it correctly

believable

Belisha beacons flashing orange lamps on black and white poles at zebra crossings, named after Leslie Hore-Belisha, the minister of transport who introduced them in 1934; have given way in many cases to pelican crossings (little red and green men)

bellringing, bellringers no hyphens

Bell's whisky

bellwether sheep that leads the herd; customarily misspelt, misused, or both

benefactor, beneficiary are sometimes confused: the former gives something; the latter gets it

benefited, benefiting

Benetton

Bengalooru formerly Bangalore

Berchtesgaden

berks and wankers

Kingsley Amis identified two principal groups in debates over use of language: "Berks are careless, coarse, crass, gross and of what anybody would agree is a lower social class than one's own; wankers are prissy, fussy, priggish, prim and of what they would probably misrepresent as a higher social class than one's own"

Bernabéu stadium the home of Real Madrid

Berne not Bern

berserk not beserk

Berwick-upon-Tweed is in England, although Berwick Rangers play football in the Scottish League

bestseller, bestselling

Betaferon TM; the generic term for the drug is **interferon-beta 1b**

bete noire no accent

betting odds

These are meaningless to many readers, and we frequently get them wrong. But here's a brief explanation: long odds (eg 100-1 against, normally expressed as 100-1) mean something unlikely; shorter odds (eg 10-1) still mean it's unlikely, but less unlikely; odds on (eg 2-1 on, sometimes expressed as 1-2) means it is likely, so if you were betting £2 you would win only £1 plus the stake.

Take care using the phrase "odds on": if Labour is quoted by bookmakers at 3-1 to win a byelection, and the odds are cut to 2-1, it is wrong to say "the odds on Labour to win were cut last night" – in fact, the odds against Labour to win have been cut (the shorter the price, the more likely something is expected to happen).

It gets more complicated when something is genuinely odds-on, ie bookmakers quote a price of "2-1 on": in this case, if the Labour candidate is quoted at 2-1 on and becomes an even hotter favourite, at 3-1 on, the odds have shortened; if Labour loses popularity, and 2-1 on becomes, say, 7-4 on or evens, the odds have lengthened

between 15 and 20 not "between 15 to 20" or "between 15-20"

Bevan, Aneurin (1897-1960) Labour health minister from 1945 to 1951 and architect of the NHS, also known as Nye Bevan

Beverly Hills

Bevin, Ernest (1881-1951) Labour foreign secretary between 1945 and 1951 who helped to create Nato

Beyoncé

biannual twice a year; **biennial** every two years; biannual is almost always misused, so to avoid confusion stick with the alternative **twice-yearly**; an alternative to biennial is **two-yearly**

bias, biased

Bible cap up if referring to Old or New Testament, lc in such sentences as "the Guardian stylebook is my bible"; the adjective **biblical** is always lc; **Bible belt**

biblical quotations

Use a modern translation, not the Authorised Version. From a reader: "Peradventure the editor hath no copy of Holy Writ in the office, save the King James Version only. Howbeit the great multitude of believers knoweth this translation not. And he (or she) who quoteth the words of Jesus in ancient form, sheweth plainly that he (or she) considereth them to be out of date. Wherefore let them be quoted in such manner that the people may understand"

biblical references Genesis 1:1; II Corinthians 2:13; Revelation 3:16 (anyone calling it "Revelations" will burn in hell for eternity)

bicentenary a 200th anniversary; **bicentennial** its adjective

biceps singular and plural (there is no such thing as a bicep)

39

bid use only in a financial or sporting sense, eg Royal Bank of Scotland has made a bid for ABN Amro, Barcelona have put in a bid for Rooney, etc; or when writing about an auction. Say "in an effort to" rather than "in a bid to"

big usually preferable to major, massive, giant, mammoth, behemoth, etc, particularly in news copy

big bang lower case, whether you are talking about the origin of the universe, around 14 billion years ago, or deregulation of the City of London in 1986

bigot, bigoted

bill lc, even when giving full name; cap up only if it becomes an act

billion one thousand million: in copy use **bn** for sums of money, quantities or inanimate objects: £10bn, 1bn litres of water; otherwise billion: 6 billion people, etc; use bn in headlines

bin Laden, Osama Bin Laden on second reference. He has been stripped of his Saudi citizenship, so can be described as Saudi-born but not as a Saudi. His organisation is known as al-Qaida ("the Base")

biodegradable

biofuel

Birds Eye TM; no apostrophe

birdwatchers also known as **birders**, not "twitchers"; they go birdwatching or birding, not "twitching"

Biro TM; say **ballpoint pen**

birthplace, birthrate, birthright

Birtwistle, Sir Harrison British composer

bishops the Right Rev Clifford Richard, Bishop of Wimbledon, at first mention; thereafter just Richard or the bishop

bismillah means "in the name of God" in Arabic

bite-size not bite-sized; very few things are the same size as a bite

bitterest use of this word by the Guardian in 2006 provoked a bitter controversy among readers, many of whom (rightly) pointed out that there is nothing wrong with it

black use only as an adjective when referring to race

blackberry fruit; plural **blackberries**

BlackBerry handheld wireless email device; plural **BlackBerrys**

Black Country

black economy prefer hidden or parallel economy

black-on-black violence is banned, unless in a quote, but even then treat with scepticism (imagine the police saying they were "investigating an incident of white-on-white violence between Millwall and West Ham supporters")

blackout

Blackpool pleasure beach a giant funfair, not a beach, so do not illustrate with a picture of donkeys on the sand

Blade Runner not Bladerunner

Blair/Booth, Cherie is **Cherie Blair** when we are referring to her in her capacity as the wife of the former prime minister; if she is appearing in court or at a function related to her work as a lawyer, she is **Cherie Booth QC** (Booth on second mention)

Blanchett, Cate

blase no accent

blastfurnace

bleeper pager; not to be confused with **beeper**, a thing that goes "beep" (eg on a microwave)

blitz, blitzkrieg

blogging

blog (noun) collection of articles, (verb) action of publishing an article to the blog: "I just blogged about that"

post (noun) single article on blog, (verb) action of publishing an article to the blog: "I was going to post later" (also: blogpost)

blogger person who authors posts (also: author)

comment text-based audience interaction with an individual blogpost

commenter audience member interacting via comments with blogposts (also: user)

comment thread list of comments following a blogpost

blond adjective and male noun; **blonde** female noun: the woman is a blonde, because she has blond hair; the man has blond hair and is, if you insist, a blond

bloodsports

bloody mary

Bloody Sunday take care when writing about the death toll: 13 died in Derry on January 30 1972, but a 14th victim died from a brain tumour several months later, so we should use a phrase such as "which led to 14 deaths"

Bluffer's Guide TM; beware of using phrases such as "a bluffer's guide to crimewriting", a headline that led to a legal complaint

Blu-ray TM; full name is Blu-ray Disc (not Disk), abbreviation BD

Blu-Tack TM

Boat Race Oxford v Cambridge

Boddingtons popularly known as Boddies, it remains the cream of Manchester, despite the closure of the Strangeways brewery

bodybuilder, bodybuilding

Bogarde, Dirk (1921-99) British actor

Bogart, Humphrey (1899-1957) American actor

bogey golf, ghost, so **bogeyman**

bogie trolley, truck

Bogotá capital of Colombia

Bombay is now known as **Mumbai**

bona fide, bona fides

Bonham Carter, Helena

bon vivant not bon viveur

boo-boo mistake

Boo Boo cartoon bear who lived with Yogi in Jellystone Park

bookcase, bookkeeper, bookseller, bookshelf

book titles are not italicised, except in the newspaper's Review section; lc for a, an, and, at, for, from, in, of, the, to (unless they are the first word of the title): A Tale of Two Cities, The Pride and the Passion, etc

bordeaux wine

bored with, bored by not bored of, although usage seems to be changing, particularly among younger people

borstals named after a village in Kent, these institutions were replaced by youth custody centres in 1982, four years after being immortalised by the Sham 69 single Borstal Breakout

bortsch

Bosphorus not Bosporus

Boston Strangler

both unnecessary in most phrases that contain "and"; "both men and women" says no more than "men and women", takes longer, and can also be ambiguous

Botox TM

bottleneck

Boudicca not Boadicea

Boundary Commission

bourgeois adjective; **bourgeoisie** noun

Boutros Boutros-Ghali former UN secretary general

box office

boy male under 18

boyband

boyfriend

Boy's Own

brackets

If the sentence is logically and grammatically complete without the information contained within the parentheses (round brackets), the punctuation stays outside the brackets.

(A complete sentence that stands alone in parentheses starts with a capital letter and ends with a stop.)

"Square brackets," the grammarian said, "are used in direct quotes when an interpolation [a note from the writer or editor, not uttered by the speaker] is added to provide essential information."

braggadocio

braille

brand avoid tabloidese such as "Mourinho brands Ferguson a liar"

Brands Hatch no apostrophe

Brasilia capital of Brazil

breastfed, breastfeeding

Bremner, Ewen actor

briar bush, pipe

bric-a-brac

brickbat only use if you know what a brickbat is

bridges lc, eg Golden Gate bridge, Waterloo bridge

Bridgnorth, Bridgwater

Brighton and Hove a city and unitary council since 2000, and no longer in East Sussex

Brink's-Mat

Britain, UK

These terms are synonymous: Britain is the official short form of United Kingdom of Great Britain and Northern Ireland. Used as adjectives, therefore, British and UK mean the same. Great Britain, however, refers only to England, Wales and Scotland.

Take care not to write Britain when you might mean only England and Wales, for example when referring to the education system *see Scotland*

Britart

British Council

British empire but British Empire Medal

British Film Institute BFI on second mention

British Library

British Medical Association (doctors' trade union), BMA on second mention

British Museum

British Sign Language abbreviate to **BSL** after first mention

Britpop

Britvic TM

Broadmoor a secure psychiatric hospital, not a prison

Brontë Charlotte, Emily, Anne and their brother Branwell; they grew up at Haworth (not Howarth) in what is now West Yorkshire

bronze age, ice age, iron age, stone age

brownie points

Brownies for girls aged seven to 10, at which point they may join the Guides

Brueghel family of Flemish painters

Brum, Brummie

brussels sprouts

brutalise render brutal, not treat brutally; so soldiers may be brutalised by the experience of war

Brylcreem TM

BSE bovine spongiform encephalopathy; no need to spell out

BST bovine somatrophin (bovine growth hormone)

BST British summer time

BTec

Buckingham Palace the palace on second mention

I take exception to the headline "Businessmen carry on flying". It should read "Business people carry on flying". I'm a business executive and I fly on business. I also happen to be a girlie.
Carol Clifton, Stone, Staffordshire

buckminsterfullerene a form of carbon, named after the US engineer Buckminster Fuller (1895-1983)

budget, the lc noun and adj, eg budget talks, budget measures, mini-budget, pre-budget report, etc

buffaloes for the plural; not buffalo or buffalos

Bulger, James not Jamie

bullseye

bumf not bumph

Buñuel, Luis (1900-83) Spanish film director

buoyed buoyed up by, not buoyed by

Burberry TM

bureau plural **bureaus** (furniture) or **bureaux** (organisations)

burgeon means to bud or sprout, so you can have someone with burgeoning talent; often misused to describe anything that is growing or expanding, especially population

burgomaster not burgomeister

burka not burqa

Burma not Myanmar

burned/burnt burned is the past tense form (he burned the cakes); burnt is the participle, an "adjectival" form of the verb ("the cakes are burnt")

Burns Night January 25

Burton upon Trent

buses, bussed, bussing

Bush, George not George W; his father is George Bush Sr

businesslike

businessman, businesswoman but say **business people** or the **business community** rather than "businessmen", which still finds its way into the paper occasionally

Bussell, Darcey Royal Ballet dancer who retired in 2007

but, however often redundant, and increasingly wrongly used to connect two compatible statements; "in contrast, however, ... " is tautologous

Butlins but **Pontin's**

butterflies and moths are usually lc: adonis blue, painted lady, red admiral, death's head hawk moth, etc; but note the following: duke of Burgundy fritillary, queen of Spain fritillary, Essex skipper, Lulworth skipper, Scotch argus

buyout but **buy-in**

byelection, bylaw, bypass, bystander

byte unit of measurement of computer information storage, eg 320GB hard drive (320 gigabytes)

> I know "bored of" is now so prevalent among the young that it is going to win the day eventually – I've been an English language specialist since the 60s and tutor an Open University course on English/linguistics – but to me, and I would guess anyone over about 40, it still sounds juvenile and uneducated.
> Liz Moloney, Eastbourne

Cc

"I am a poet. I distrust anything
that starts with a capital letter
and ends with a full stop."
Antjie Krog

cabby not cabbie but plural **cabbies**

cabin attendant, flight attendant, cabin crew, cabin staff not air hostess, stewardess

cabinet, shadow cabinet

caddie golf; **caddy** tea

Cádiz

Caernarfon place; **Lord Carnarvon** person

caesar salad

caesarean section

Caesars Palace no apostrophe

Cafcass Children and Family Court Advisory and Support Service

cafe no accent

Calcutta now **Kolkata**

Californian a person; the adjective is California, or Brian Wilson would have written about "Californian Girls"; the same rule applies to other US states, so a "Texan drilling for Texas tea" is an oilman

call girl old-fashioned term best left to the Sunday tabloids

Calor TM

Campari TM

Canal+ French TV channel, formerly Canal Plus

Canary Wharf the whole development, not the main tower, which is 1 Canada Square

Cancún city in Mexico

cannabis people smoke cannabis rather than "experiment" with it, despite what politicians and young members of the royal family might claim

canon cleric, decree, principle, body of writings, type of music; a **cannon** is something you fire

Canute (c994-1035) Danish king of England, Denmark and Norway who commanded the tide to turn back, so the legend says – not in a vain attempt to exercise power over nature, but to prove to his toadying courtiers that he was not all-powerful (lots of people get this wrong)

canvas tent, painting; **canvass** solicit votes

CAP common agricultural policy

capitals

Times have changed since the days of medieval manuscripts with elaborate hand-illuminated capital letters, or Victorian documents in which not just proper names, but virtually all nouns, were given initial caps (a Tradition valiantly maintained to this day by Estate Agents).

A look through newspaper archives would show greater use of capitals the further back you went. The tendency towards lower case, which in part reflects a less formal, less deferential society, has been accelerated by the explosion of the internet: some net companies, and many email users, have dispensed with capitals altogether.

Our style reflects these developments. We aim for coherence and consistency, but not at the expense of clarity. As with any aspect of style, it is impossible to be wholly consistent – there are almost always exceptions, so if you are unsure check for an individual entry in this guide. But here are the main principles:

jobs all lc, eg prime minister, US secretary of state, editor of the Guardian, readers' editor.

titles cap up titles, but not job description, eg the Archbishop of Canterbury, the Right Rev Rowan Williams, at first mention, thereafter Williams or the archbishop; President George Bush (but the US president, George Bush, and Bush on subsequent mention); the Duke of Westminster (the duke at second mention); the Pope; the Queen.

British government departments of state initial caps, eg Home Office, Foreign Office, Ministry of Justice *see departments of state for a full list*

other countries' departments of state lc, eg US state department, Russian foreign ministry.

government agencies, public bodies, quangos initial caps, eg Commission for Equality and Human Rights, Crown Prosecution Service, Heritage Lottery Fund, Revenue & Customs.

acts of parliament initial caps (but bills lc), eg Official Secrets Act, Criminal Justice Act 1992.

parliamentary committees, reports and inquiries all lc, eg trade and industry select committee, Lawrence report, royal commission on electoral reform.

artistic and cultural names of institutions, etc, get initial caps, eg British Museum, National Gallery, Royal Albert Hall, Tate Modern. Books, films, music, works of art, etc have initial caps except a, an, and, at, for, from, in, of, the, to (except in initial positions or after a colon).

churches, hospitals and schools cap up the proper or placename, lc the rest, eg St Peter's church, Pembury; Great Ormond Street children's hospital; Ripon grammar school; Vernon county infants school.

universities and colleges of further and higher education caps for institution, lc for departments, eg Sheffield University department of medieval and modern history, Oregon State University, Free University of Berlin, University of Queensland school of journalism, London College of Communication.

airports, bridges cap the name but lc the generic part (if necessary at all), eg Heathrow, Gatwick (no need for "airport"), Liverpool John Lennon airport, Golden Gate bridge, Waterloo bridge, etc

geographical features lc, eg river Thames, Sydney harbour, Monterey peninsula, Bondi beach, Solsbury hill (but Mount Everest).

words and phrases based on proper names that have lost connection with their origins (alsatian, cardigan, champagne, cheddar cheese, cornish pasty, french windows, wellington boots, yorkshire pudding and numerous others) are usually lc; many are listed individually in this guide, as are exceptions (eg Parma ham, Worcestershire sauce)

cappuccino

car bomb, car park but **carmaker**

carcass plural **carcasses**

cards: scratchcard, smartcard, swipecard but **credit card, debit card, sim card**

careen to sway or keel over to one side; often confused with **career**, to rush along

career girl, career woman these labels are banned

carer an unpaid family member, partner or friend who helps a disabled or frail person with the activities of daily living; not someone who works in a caring job or profession. The term is important because carers are entitled to a range of benefits and services that depend on them recognising themselves as carers

Cc

Caribbean
– CD

Caribbean

cash for honours noun; **cash-for-honours** adjective

cashmere fabric

caster sugar, wheels on a sofa; **castor** oil

castoff one word (noun, adjective); **cast off** two words (verb)

casual (workers) freelance is often preferable

casualties includes dead and injured, so not a synonym for deaths

casualty lc, as in she's been taken to casualty (though normally called A&E)

Catalonia adjective **Catalan**

catch-22 lc unless specifically referring to Joseph Heller's novel Catch-22

catchphrase

cathedrals cap up, eg Canterbury Cathedral

catherine wheel

Catholic church

caviar not caviare

CBeebies

CD, CDs, CD-Rom a CD is a disc, not a disk

CE common era, current era or Christian era: some people prefer this expression (and **BCE**, for "before common era", etc) to AD and BC, which, however, remain our style

ceasefire

Ceausescu, Nicolae former president of Romania, deposed and executed in 1989

ceilidh

celibate, celibacy strictly refer to being unmarried (especially for religious reasons), but it is now acceptable to use them to mean abstaining from sexual intercourse

celsius without degree symbol and with fahrenheit equivalent in brackets: 23C (73F), -3C (27F), etc; to convert celsius to fahrenheit, multiply by 9, divide by 5, then add 32; to convert fahrenheit to celsius, subtract 32, divide the answer by 9, then multiply by 5 (or use one of the many online calculators)

Celtic not Glasgow Celtic

cement or **concrete**? not interchangeable terms: cement is an ingredient of concrete, which is a mix of aggregates (sand and gravel or crushed stone) and paste (water and portland cement); so a "cement mixer" should always be referred to as a concrete mixer

censor prevent publication; **censure** criticise severely

Center Parcs

central belt the swath across Scotland, containing Glasgow and Edinburgh, where population density is highest. It is in the south, not the centre of the country

centre on or in; **revolve** around

Centre Court Wimbledon

century sixth century, 21st century, etc; but sixth-century remains, 21st-century boy, etc

Cern the Geneva-based European laboratory for particle physics

Cézanne, Paul (1839-1906) French artist

CFC chlorofluorocarbon

chablis wines are lc, whether named after a place (as in this case) or a grape variety

cha-cha-cha the dance, not cha-cha

chair acceptable in place of chairman or chairwoman, being nowadays widely used in the public sector and by organisations such as the Labour party and trade unions (though not the Conservative party, which had a "chairman" in kitten heels); if it seems inappropriate for a particular body, use a different construction ("the meeting was chaired by Alan" or "Georgina was in the chair")

champagne

Champs Elysées

chancellor of the duchy of Lancaster

chancellor of the exchequer

changeable

Channel, the

Channel 4, Channel Five but **Five** at second mention

Channel Islands

Channel tunnel not Chunnel

chaos theory not a synonym for chaos. It describes the behaviour of dynamic systems that are sensitively dependent on their initial conditions. An example is the weather: under the "butterfly effect", the flap of a butterfly's wing in Brazil can in principle result in a tornado in Texas

chardonnay lc, like other wines, whether named after a grape (as in this case) or a region

chargé, chargée d'affaires

Charity Commission

Chartered Institute of Public Finance and Accountancy
Cipfa or the institute after first mention

chassis singular and plural

chateau, chateaux no accent

Chatham House rule often mistakenly called "rules". There is just one, namely: "When a meeting, or part thereof, is held under the Chatham House rule, participants are free to use the information received, but neither the identity nor the affiliation of the speaker(s), nor that of any other participant, may be revealed."
 Chatham House is more formally known as the Royal Institute of International Affairs, based at Chatham House in London

chatroom, chatshow

Chávez, Hugo

chavs avoid

Chechnya inhabited by **Chechens**

checkout noun, adjective; **check out** verb

cheese normally lc, even if named after a place: **brie, camembert, cheddar, cheshire, double gloucester, lancashire, parmesan, stilton, wensleydale**, etc

Chek Lap Kok Hong Kong international airport, designed by Sir Norman Foster, opened in 1998

Chennai formerly Madras

chequebook

cherubim plural of cherub

Cheshire cat but **cheshire cheese**

chickenpox one word

chicken tikka masala Britain's favourite dish; note that there is also an Italian dish called **chicken marsala**

chief ("planning chiefs", etc): try to use proper titles; officers or officials may be preferable

chief constable a job, not a title – John Smith, chief constable of Greater Manchester; Smith at second mention

chief secretary to the Treasury

chief whip

childcare, childminder

ChildLine

child trust fund colloquially known as baby bonds

Chinese names

Mainland China: in two parts, eg Mao Zedong, Zhou Enlai, Jiang Zemin.

Hong Kong, Taiwan: in two parts with hyphen, eg Tung Chee-hwa, Chiang Kai-shek (exception: when a building, park or the like is named after a person it becomes three parts, eg Chiang Kai Shek Cultural Centre); note also that Korean names are written the same way, eg Kim Il-sung.

Singapore, Malaysia: in three parts, eg Lee Kuan Yew.

For people with Chinese names elsewhere in the world, follow their preference – but make sure you know which is the surname

Chloé (fashion) not Chloë

chock-a-block

chocoholic not chocaholic

Chomsky, Noam US linguist

choose for some strange reason this often appears as "chose", its past tense

chords musical; **cords** vocal

christened, christening use only when referring to a Christian baptism: don't talk about a boat being christened or a football club christening a new stadium; **named** is fine

Christian, Christianity but **unchristian**

Christian name use first name, forename or given name (in many cultures, it comes after the family name)

Christian Union an evangelical Christian organisation

Christie's

Christmas Day, Christmas Eve

chronic means lasting for a long time or constantly recurring, too often misused when acute (short but severe) is meant

Chumbawamba not Chumbawumba

church lc for the established church, eg "the church is no longer relevant today"; Catholic church, Anglican church, etc, but Church of England

cineaste someone who enjoys films; but note that, in France, a *cinéaste* is someone who makes them

cinemagoer

Cites convention on international trade in endangered species of wild fauna and flora

Citizens Advice what the organisation likes to be called, although it still runs bureaux

Citroën

city in Britain a town that has been granted a charter by the crown; it usually has a cathedral

City capped when used as shorthand for the City of London

civil partnership rather than gay marriage, but gay wedding is fine and does not need quotation marks

civil servant, civil service

CJD Creutzfeldt-Jakob disease, not normally necessary to spell it out; it is acceptable to refer to variant CJD as the human form of BSE, but not "the human form of mad cow disease"

classical music Mozart's 41st Symphony (or Symphony No 41) in C, K551; Rachmaninov's Piano Concerto No 2; Schubert's Sonata in A minor for Piano, D845

clearcut

cliches

Overused words and phrases to be avoided, some of which merit their own ignominious entry in this book, include: back burner, boost (massive or otherwise), bouquets and brickbats, but hey ... , count 'em, debt mountain, drop-dead gorgeous, elephant in the room, fit for purpose, insisted, key, major, massive, meanwhile, politically correct, raft of measures, special, to die for, upsurge; verbs overused in headlines include: bid, boost, fuel, hike, signal, spiral, target, set to.

A survey by the Plain English Campaign found that the most irritating phrase in the language was "at the end of the day", followed by (in order of annoyance): at this moment in time, like (as in, like, this), with all due respect, to be perfectly honest with you, touch base, I hear what you're saying, going forward, absolutely, and blue sky thinking; other words and phrases that upset people included 24/7, ballpark figure, bottom line, diamond geezer, it's not rocket science, ongoing, prioritise, pushing the envelope, singing from the same hymn sheet, and thinking outside the box

cliffhanger

climbdown noun; **climb down** verb

clingfilm

Close, Glenn two Ns (as in bunny boiler)

cloud cuckoo land

coalfield, coalmine, coalminer

Coalite TM

coarse fishing we have been known to spell it "course"

coastguard

Coca-Cola, Coke TM; the generic term is **cola**

cockney

coconut

cold war

Coliseum London theatre; **Colosseum** Rome

collectible

collective nouns

Nouns such as committee, family, government, jury and squad take a singular verb or pronoun when thought of as a single unit, but a plural verb or pronoun when thought of as a collection of individuals:

The committee gave its unanimous approval to the plans;
The committee enjoyed biscuits with their tea
The family can trace its history back to the middle ages;
The family were sitting down, scratching their heads

collector's item

College of Arms

colleges take initial caps, eg London College of Communication; but not when college forms part of the name of a school, eg Bash Street sixth-form college, Eton college

Colombia South American country that we frequently misspell as "Columbia"

colon

Use between two sentences, or parts of sentences, where the first introduces a proposition that is resolved by the second, eg Fowler put it like this: to deliver the goods invoiced in the preceding words.

A colon should also be used (rather than a comma) to introduce a quotation: "He was an expert on punctuation," or to precede a list – "He was an expert on the following: the colon, the comma and the full stop."

This, from the paper, is a dreadful (but by no means isolated) example of the tendency to use a semicolon where only a colon will do: "Being a retired soap 'treasure' must be a bit like being in the army reserves; when a ratings war breaks out, it's time to dust off your uniform and wait by the phone."

We are in danger of losing the distinction between colon and semicolon; many writers seem to think they are interchangeable but to make it clear: they are not *see semicolon*

colonel Colonel Napoleon Bogey, subsequently Bogey

Columbia as in District of Columbia (Washington DC) and Columbia University (New York)

Columbus Day October 12, marking the date Christopher Columbus landed in the West Indies in 1492; Columbus is also the state capital of Ohio

Can we establish yet again that a centre is a fixed point and that therefore a story cannot "centre around" something, only "centre on"? By all means "circle around" but let's not go round in circles on this point.

Tony Barlow, Wallington, Surrey

65

comedian male and female; do not use comedienne

commas

"The editor, Alan Rusbridger, is a man of great vision" – correct (commas) if there is only one.

"The subeditor David Marsh is all style and no substance" – correct (no commas) if there are more than one.

A misplaced comma can sabotage a sentence, as in this example from the paper: "Neocon economists often claim a large, black economy turbo-powers growth ... " (the writer meant a big black economy, not a big and black one, which is not the same at all)

commented "said" is normally adequate

Commission for Equality and Human Rights body created in 2007 to bring together the work of the Commission for Racial Equality, the Disability Rights Commission, and the Equal Opportunities Commission; may be called CEHR, or simply the commission, after first mention

common agricultural policy lc but the abbreviation is CAP

Commons, House of Commons but the house, not the House

Commons committees lc, home affairs select committee, public accounts committee, etc

common sense noun; **commonsense** adjective: "William Hague's 'commonsense revolution' showed little common sense"

Commonwealth, the

Commonwealth War Graves Commission

communique no accent

communism, communist lc, except in name of party:
Communist party

community charge what no one, apart from a handful of
Conservative ministers, called the poll tax

company names

A difficult area, as so many companies these days have adopted
unconventional typography and other devices that, in some cases,
turn their names into logos. In general, we use the names that
companies use themselves: c2c, Capgemini, easyJet, eBay, ebookers,
iSoft Group, etc.

Exceptions include Adidas (not adidas), ABN Amro (not ABN
AMRO), BAE Systems (not BAE SYSTEMS), BhS (no italicised H),
Toys R Us (do not attempt to turn the R backwards), Yahoo (no
exclamation mark). See individual entries for more examples.

Many of these look odd, particularly when used as the first word
in a headline, although some are becoming more familiar with time

compare to/with

The former means liken to, the latter means make a comparison: so
unless you are specifically likening someone or something to someone
or something else (eg Nothing Compares 2 U), use compare with.

The lord chancellor compared himself to Cardinal Wolsey because
he believed he was like Wolsey; I might compare him with Wolsey to
assess their relative merits.

compass points lc for regions: the north, the south of
England, the south-west, north-east Scotland, south Wales; the
same applies to geopolitical areas: the west, western Europe, the
far east, south-east Asia, central America, etc; cap up, however,

when part of the name of a county (West Sussex, East Riding of Yorkshire) or province (East Java, North Sulawesi, etc); note the following: East End, West End (London), Middle East, Latin America, North America, South America

Competition Commission

complement/compliment/complimentary to complement is to make complete: the two strikers complemented each other; to compliment is to praise; a complimentary copy is free

complete or **finish** is better than finalise

comprise to consist of; "comprise of" is wrong

Concord town in Massachusetts; **Concorde** plane

congestion charge

Congo acceptable on second mention for the Democratic Republic of the Congo (or DRC, formerly Zaire); we call its neighbour **Congo-Brazzaville**; never write "the Congo" unless referring to the river

Congregational uc when referring to the Congregational Union of England and Wales, formed in 1832, which joined the Presbyterian Church of England in 1972 to form the United Reformed Church

Congress comprises the House of Representatives (the house) and Senate; but lc congressman, congresswoman, congressional

conjoined twins not Siamese twins

connection not connexion

Conservative central office

Conservative party

consortium plural **consortiums**

constitution

Consuelo not Consuela; from a reader: "I really have had
enough of show-off ignoramuses messing up my name.
Consuelo is a Spanish abstract noun, masculine, invariable. Pilar
and Mercedes are also Spanish female names derived, like
Consuelo, from titles of the Virgin Mary"

consult not consult with

consumer price index (CPI) normally no need to spell it out

Consumers' Association

contemporary of the same period, though often wrongly used
to mean modern; a performance of Shakespeare in
contemporary dress would involve Elizabethan costume, not
21st-century clothes

continent, the mainland Europe

continual refers to things that happen repeatedly but not
constantly; **continuous** indicates an unbroken sequence

contractions Do not overuse contractions such as aren't, can't,
couldn't, hasn't, don't, I'm, it's, there's and what's (even the
horrific "there've" has appeared in the paper); while they might
make a piece more colloquial or easier to read, they can be an
irritant and a distraction, and make a serious article sound
frivolous. They also look horrible

controversial overused, typically to show that the writer
disapproves of something ("the government's controversial
academy schools scheme"); like "famous", it can normally be
safely removed from copy to allow readers to make up their
own minds

convener not convenor

conversions

We give metric measures and convert on first mention only to imperial in brackets (exceptions: miles and pints); if a rough figure is given in metric, do not convert it into an exact figure in imperial, and vice versa, eg if someone says the towns are about 50km apart, convert to 30 miles, not "31.07 miles"; the same goes for rough amounts of currencies, though don't round up £3.6bn to £4bn

convertible not -able

convince/persuade having convinced someone of the facts, you might persuade them to do something

Co-op store (although it calls itself Co-Op)

cooperate, cooperation, cooperative no hyphen

coordinate

copy editor what subeditors are known as in the United States, where they **copy-edit**; books are also copy-edited

copyright but **copywriter**

Corbusier, Le (1887-1965) Swiss architect and city planner, born Charles-Edouard Jeanneret

cords vocal; **chords** musical

Córdoba

cornflakes in general but **Kellogg's Corn Flakes**

cornish pasty

coronavirus

corporation of London

corps de ballet

cortege no accent

coruscating means sparkling, or emitting flashes of light; people seem to think, wrongly, that it means the same as **excoriating**, censuring severely, eg "a coruscating attack on Brown's advisers"

cosmetic surgery is not the same as **plastic surgery**, which should be reserved for people treated for deformity or illness

councils lc apart from placename: Lancaster city council, Southwark borough council, Kent county council; it is normally sufficient to say Lancaster council, Southwark council, etc

count 'em resist the temptation to use this cliche, often seen in parenthesis after a number is mentioned. For example, an article referred to "the seminal Andrex puppy advent calendar with 25 – count 'em – puppy pictures ..."

counteract, counterattack, countermeasures

coupe no accent

courts all lc, eg court of appeal, court of session, high court, magistrates court (no apostrophe), supreme court, European court of human rights, international criminal court

court martial plural **courts martial**

court of St James's

couscous

CPRE Campaign to Protect Rural England (formerly the Council for the Protection of Rural England)

Cradock, Fanny (1909-94) TV chef, often misspelt as "Craddock"

creche no accent

credibility capable of being believed; **credulity** gullibility; we sometimes mix the two up

creme fraiche

crescendo a gradual increase in loudness or intensity; musically or figuratively, it is the build-up to a climax, not the climax itself (we frequently get this wrong)

cricket leg-side, leg-spinner, off-spin, off-stump, silly mid-on, mid-off, etc, all hyphenated

cripple, crippled offensive and outdated; do not use

crisscross

criterion plural **criteria**

Crombie TM

Crowley, Aleister dead satanist

crown, the crown estate, crown jewels

crucifix not synonymous with cross: a crucifix depicts the body of Christ on the cross

crucifixion, the

Crufts

cruise missile

Crusades, the

Cruz, Penélope

cubism, cubist

Cub scouts boys (and now girls) aged from eight to 10, organised in packs but no longer known as "Wolf Cubs"; avoid dated "Dyb Dyb Dyb, Dob Dob Dob" jokes but if relevant, it is spelt thus (it stands for "do your best" and we will "do our best"), and not "Dib"

cull means pick or choose as in "culled from the best authors". It doesn't mean killed, axed or massacred (though you cull sheep in order to kill them). So a jobs cull does not mean the same as mass sackings

cumberland sausage

Cummings, EE US poet (1894-1962) who, despite what many people think, used capitals in his signature

Cup, FA after first mention it is the Cup; but other cups are lc on second mention

curb restrain; **kerb** pavement

currencies

When the whole word is used it is lc: euro, pound, sterling, dong, etc.
    Abbreviate dollars like this: $50 (US dollars); A$50 (Australian dollars); HK$50 (Hong Kong dollars).

Convert all foreign amounts to sterling in brackets at first mention, but use common sense — there is no need to put £500,000 in brackets after the phrase "I feel like a million dollars."

Take care when converting old money to new: some of our attempts have been meaningless, in that they have ignored the relative value of sums involved. We said in an obituary, for example, that Ronnie Barker was paid £1 9s (£1.45) a week for his first job in 1947 — a comparison of average earnings would convert that to around £113 today.

Similarly, in converting the price of a "four shilling dish of rice and vegetables" in 1967 to 20p in today's money we forgot to allow for its relative value; taking into account changes in the retail price index it would now be worth £2.23.

There are some excellent websites to assist with such conversions

currently "now" is usually preferable, if needed at all

cusp a place where two points meet (eg "on the cusp of Manchester and Salford", "on the cusp of Taurus and Gemini"), which may be extended metaphorically to a place or time where two things or groups of things come into contact, as in this elegant example from the Review: "It was a world caught on the cusp between postwar recession, stasis and a dying moral code, and the colour, mobility and licence of the 60s."

Writers who use cusp under the impression that it is a clever way to say on the brink of or about to ("on the cusp of adolescence", "on the cusp of the final", "the garlic was on the cusp of bursting into a constellation of white stars") are, sadly, mistaken

custody since the 1989 Children Act the correct term for what used to be known as custody in cases involving care of children is **residence**

Customs, Revenue & Customs (singular) but **customs officers**

cutbacks avoid; **cuts** will suffice

cyberspace

Cyprus Cyprus, properly known as the Republic of Cyprus, joined the EU in 2004, 30 years after Turkey invaded the northern part of the island, which should be referred to as "Turkish-occupied northern Cyprus" (the self-styled "Turkish Republic of Northern Cyprus" is recognised only by Turkey)

Czech Republic

Can nothing be done to stop your writers using the pretentious journalists' phrase "ahead of"? Surely it isn't approved of by the Guardian stylebook? Raymond Briggs recently said on Radio 4 that the refusal to use direct, simple words such as "before" made him want to throw his radio at the wall. Throwing my Guardian at the wall offers little relief. The phrase is scattered throughout most editions. You could scour the newspaper to find a writer using "before".

Michael Bateson, Louth, Lincolnshire

Dd

"Leave the rooster story alone –
that's human interest!"
**Ben Hecht and Charles
MacArthur, The Front Page**

Dad or **dad**? I'll have to ask Dad, then you can check with your dad

dadaism, dadaist

Dáil Éireann lower house of parliament in the Irish Republic, normally just the Dáil

DaimlerChrysler

Dalí, Salvador (1904-89) Spanish surrealist

dancefloor

dangling participles

Avoid constructions such as "having died, they buried him"; the pitfalls are nicely highlighted in Mark Lawson's novel Going Out Live, in which a TV critic writes: "Dreary, repetitive and well past the sell-by date, I switched off the new series of Fleming Faces."

A particularly exotic example of this that somehow found its way into the Guardian: "Though long-legged and possessing a lovely smile, gentleman journalists aren't looking up her skirt and wouldn't even if she weren't gay ... "

dark ages

dashes

Beware sentences – such as this one – that dash about all over the place – commas (or even, very occasionally, brackets) are often better; semicolons also have their uses

data takes a singular verb (like agenda); though strictly a plural, no one ever uses "agendum" or "datum"

dates

Our style is July 21 2008 (no commas), and has been since the first issue of the Manchester Guardian on May 5 1821 (it is occasionally alleged that putting month before date in this way is an "Americanisation").

In the 21st century but 21st-century boy; fourth century BC; AD2007, 2500BC, 10,000BC; for decades use figures: the swinging 60s or 1960s

daughter of, son of

Think twice before using these terms. Often only the person's father is described and such descriptions can smack of snobbery as well as sexism. Simplistic labels may also be misleading: we published a clarification after calling Captain James Cook the son of a Scottish farm labourer. True enough, but Cook's mother was a Yorkshire woman and he is a famous son of Yorkshire

Davison, Emily suffragette who died four days after stepping in front of George V's horse at the 1913 Derby

daybreak, daydream

Day-Glo TM

daylong but **month-long, year-long**

daytime but **night-time**

day trip two words, as in the Beatles' Day Tripper

D-day

deaf ears avoid or say "closed ears": the phrase is not just a rather lazy cliche but offensive to many deaf people; for the same reason, do not use "dialogue of the deaf"; most deaf

Dd

deathbed
– delphic

people are perfectly capable of conducting a dialogue using BSL and other sign languages

deathbed but **death row**

debacle no accents; like farce and fiasco, to be used sparingly in news reporting

debatable

decades 1950s, etc; use figures if you abbreviate: roaring 20s, swinging 60s, a woman in her 70s, the first reader's email of the 00s

decimate nowadays used to mean destroy *see Latin*

declarations lc, eg Lacken declaration on the future of Europe

deep south of the US

defensible

defuse render harmless; **diffuse** spread about

Degas, Edgar (1834-1917) French artist; no accents

de Gaulle, Charles (1890-1970) French military leader and statesman; De Gaulle on second mention

degrees like this: my sons all got firsts, but I only got a second – although it was a 2:1 – and I did go on to a master's

deja vu no accents

Deloitte not Deloittes, Deloitte Consulting, or Deloitte & Touche

delphic

80

delusion or **illusion**? "That the sun moves round the Earth was once a delusion, and is still an illusion"(Fowler)

DeMille, Cecil B (1881-1959) Hollywood producer and director

Democratic party not "Democrat party", despite attempts by some Republicans to call it this

Dench, Dame Judi not Judy

denier one who denies, as in "Holocaust denier"; also a unit of weight for fibre, eg 10-denier tights

De Niro, Robert

denouement no accent

departments of state

British government ministries (but not ministers) take initial caps, as follows:

Cabinet Office (but **the cabinet**)

Home Office

Foreign Office (abbreviate to FCO – for Foreign and Commonwealth Office – after first mention)

Treasury

Department for Business, Enterprise and Regulatory Reform (DBERR)

Department for Children, Schools and Families (DCSF)

Communities and Local Government

Department for Culture, Media and Sport (DCMS)

Department for Environment, Food and Rural Affairs (Defra)

Department for Innovation, Universities and Skills (Dius)

Department for International Development (DfID)

Department for Transport (DfT)

Department for Work and Pensions (DWP)

Department of Health (DH)

Ministry of Defence (MoD)

Ministry of Justice (MoJ)

Office of the Leader of the House of Commons

Northern Ireland Office

Scotland Office not Scottish Office

Wales Office not Welsh Office

Use the abbreviations in brackets sparingly, especially the clumsy ones: culture and sport department, innovation and skills department, and so on are fine, or just the department, the ministry, etc.

The rebranded Communities and Local Government is tricky, having decided to drop "Department" from its name: if we say, for example, "Communities and Local Government yesterday announced a shakeup in council tax" it makes us sound equally silly, so best to call it the communities and local government department (lc) or just communities department or local government department, depending on the story.

Departments and ministries of other countries are lc, eg US state department, Iraqi foreign ministry

dependant noun; **dependent** adjective

dependence

depositary person; **depository** place

deprecate express disapproval; **depreciate** reduce in value

de rigueur the two Us are de rigueur

derring-do not daring-do

Derry, Co Derry not Londonderry

descendants come after ancestors; you wouldn't think the Guardian would get this simple thing wrong as often as we do

deselect

desiccated not dessicated

despoil, despoliation

dessert pudding, but **just deserts**

detente

Dettol TM

developing countries use this term in preference to third world

devil, the

de Villepin, Dominique on second mention just Villepin

DeVito, Danny

Diabetes UK formerly known as the British Diabetic Association

Diaghilev, Sergei (1872-1929) Russian impresario; founder of the Ballets Russes

dialects cockney, estuary English, geordie, scouse

diaspora

DiCaprio, Leonardo

Dictaphone TM

diehard but the film series is Die Hard

dietitian must be trained and qualified in dietetics, and registered with the Health Professionals Council; not the same as a nutritionist, a less precise term (although some nutritionists are also registered dietitians)

different from or **to**, not different than

digital rights management can be abbreviated to **DRM** after first mention

dignitary, dignitaries

dilapidated not delapidated

dilettante

dim sum

"Disabled" is a label that hurts, no matter how convenient it may be to editors and writers. True, it is a sociological label, one embedded so deeply in our language (and law) that far too many people feel they must repeat it, but there is no compulsion to do so. Imagine that each day of your life you were forced to face that label, exactly as we once forced black people, with labels on every aspect of their being – restrooms, restaurants, hotels, seating on a bus – to do the same. Imagine that, forced to endure the label, you became inured to it and applied it to yourself, became it, and you will have some understanding of how words hurt, how deeply they hurt, and how difficult it is to escape the pain.

Harold Maio, Fort Myers, Florida

Dinky Toys TM

diphtheria

diplomatic service

director general

direct speech

People we write about are allowed to speak in their own, not necessarily the Guardian's, style, but be sensitive: do not, for example, expose someone to ridicule for dialect or grammatical errors. Do not attempt facetious phonetic renditions such as "oop north", "fooking" and "booger" when interviewing someone from the north, or "dahn sarf" when writing about south London

disabled people not "the disabled"

Use positive language about disability, avoiding outdated terms that stereotype or stigmatise. Terms to avoid, with acceptable alternatives in brackets, include victim of, suffering from, afflicted by, crippled by (prefer person who has, person with); wheelchair-bound, in a wheelchair (uses a wheelchair); invalid (disabled person); mentally handicapped, backward, retarded, slow (person with learning difficulties); the disabled, the handicapped, the blind, the deaf (disabled people, blind people, deaf people); deaf and dumb (deaf and speech-impaired, hearing and speech-impaired)

disc rotating optical disc: CD, CD-Rom, DVD, etc; **disk** rotating magnetic disc: disk drive, floppy disk

discernible not discernable

discharged a patient is discharged, not released, from hospital; a prisoner is released from jail

discolour but **discoloration**

discomfit thwart, readily confused with **discomfort**, make uncomfortable

discreet circumspect; **discrete** separate

disfranchise not disenfranchise

disinterested means free from bias, objective (the negative form of interested as in "interested party"); often used incorrectly instead of **uninterested**, not taking an interest (the negative form of interested as in "interested in football")

Disneyland (California), **Disneyland Paris** (formerly Euro Disney), **Disney World** (Florida)

dispatch, dispatch box (Commons), **dispatched**; not despatch, despatched

Disprin TM; use aspirin

dissociate, dissociation not disassociate, disassociation

distributor not distributer

ditching not a synonym for crashing: if you ditch a helicopter, you make a controlled landing on the water after an emergency – we have got this wrong several times

divorcee a divorced person, male or female

D notices issued by the defence, press and broadcasting advisory committee, "suggesting" that the media do not publish sensitive information

Doctor Who the title of the series; the character's name is **the Doctor**, and it should never be abbreviated to Dr Who

docudrama, docusoap

dogs lc, alsatian, doberman, rottweiler, yorkshire terrier; but Irish setter, old English sheepdog

D'oh! as Homer Simpson would say (note the apostrophe)

Dolby TM

doll's house

dome, the Millennium Dome at first mention, thereafter the dome; now **the O2**

Domesday Book but **doomsday scenario**

Dominica lies in the Windward Islands, south-west of the Dominican Republic

Dominican Republic shares the island of Hispaniola with Haiti

doner kebab *see kebabs*

donor gives money

doppelganger no accent

Doran, Seán former artistic director of English National Opera

dos and don'ts

Dostoevsky, Fyodor Mikhailovich (1821-81) Russian novelist

dotcom

double, the as in Sheffield United may win the double (FA Cup and Premiership)

dover sole

Dow Jones industrial average

downmarket, upmarket

downplay play down is preferable

Down's syndrome say (if relevant) a baby with Down's syndrome, not "a Down's syndrome baby" – we wouldn't say "a cerebral palsy baby". The diagnosis is not the person

down under don't use to refer to Australia or New Zealand

dozen precisely, not approximately, 12

Dr use at first mention for medical and scientific doctors and doctors of divinity (not, for example, a politician who happens to have a PhD in history); thereafter, just use surname except in leading articles

draconian

draftsman of document; **draughtsman** of drawing

dreamed not dreamt

dressing room two words

drier, dryer this shirt will only get drier after an hour in the tumble dryer (while I use the hairdryer)

drink past tense **drank**, past participle **drunk**: he drinks, he drank, he has sunk

drink-driver, drink-driving, drunk-driving

guardian style

driving licence not driver's licence

drone honeybee whose function is to mate with the queen, and by extension therefore someone who lives off the work of others (the worker bees); however, it seems to be used increasingly to mean something like an obedient, unimaginative worker ("office drone")

drug companies, drug dealer, drug raid, drug squad, drug tsar not drugs raid, etc

drug use a more accurate and less judgmental term than "drug abuse" or "misuse" (often all three terms have been scattered randomly through the same reports)

druid

drum'n'bass

drunkenness

DSG International formerly Dixons; owns Currys and PC World (Dixons should now only be seen on the internet)

dub avoid such tabloidese as "he has been dubbed the nation's leading expert on style" (even if true)

duct tape not duck tape

due to

Traditionalists argue that rent may be due to the landlord, but unless it is the complement of the verb "to be", "due to" should otherwise be replaced by "because of"; thus:

"The train was late due to leaves on the line" is wrong;

"The train was late because of leaves on the line" is correct;

"The train's late arrival was due to leaves on the line" is also correct.

A rough and ready test is that "due to" is fine if it can be replaced by "caused by", but not when it can be replaced by "because of".

This distinction, once routinely taught in primary schools but now assailed on all sides, especially by train and tube announcers, is being lost

dugout

Duke of Westminster or wherever, first mention; thereafter the duke

Duke of York first mention; thereafter Prince Andrew or the prince

dumb do not use when you mean **speech-impaired**

du Pré, Jacqueline (1945-87) English cellist, Du Pré at second mention

Dupré, Marcel (1886-1971) French organist and composer

dutch courage

DVD stands for digital versatile disc

dwarves plural of dwarf (not dwarfs); but the verb is to dwarf, eg 1 Canada Square dwarfs the surrounding buildings

dyke not dike

dynamo plural **dynamos**

Dynamo football teams from the former Soviet Union are Dynamo; teams from Romania are **Dinamo**

dyslexia write "Paul has dyslexia" rather than labelling him "a dyslexic" or saying he "suffers from" dyslexia

Ee

"Some editors are failed writers,
but so are most writers."

TS Eliot

Ee

EADS European Aeronautic Defence and Space Company, but no need to spell out; the group includes the aircraft manufacturer Airbus and is the major partner in the Eurofighter consortium

earlier often redundant: "they met this week" is preferable to "they met earlier this week" and will save space; "earlier this month" occurs almost every time we publish a paper on the first of the month, when it should, of course, be "last month"

Earls Court no apostrophe

earned not earnt

earring

earshot

Earth in an astronomical or science fiction context; but moon, sun

East Anglia

east Asia or **south-east Asia** rather than far east

east coast mainline

East End inner east London north of the river (the equivalent district south of the Thames is south-east London)

EastEnders TV soap

Easter Day not Easter Sunday

eastern Europe, western Europe

East Jerusalem

East Riding of Yorkshire council

easyJet

eBay

Ebola virus

ebook electronic book

ebookers online travel company

eccles cake

E coli as with other taxonomic names, italicise in copy but roman in headlines and standfirsts; no full point

e-commerce

ecosystem, ecowarrior

ecstasy (drug), lc

ecu European currency unit, superseded by the euro

Edinburgh festival, Edinburgh Fringe festival

editor lc: editor of the Guardian, editor of the Redditch Indicator series, etc

educationist not educationalist

eerie weird; **Erie** North American lake; **eyrie** of eagles

effect/affect *see affect*

effectively is not a synonym for in effect: "the Brown campaign was effectively launched in 2007" means the launch was official and its intended effect was achieved; "the Brown campaign was in effect launched in 1997" means this was not the official launch, but events at the time described did have the effect of

Every time I read the word "Gallic" in the UK press, there follows some ludicrous generalisation about what French people do or are like. I would recommend that any writer, when tempted to use the word, should check what they are writing for stereotyping and prejudiced blather. The equivalent for Germany is of course "Teutonic".

Sam Featherston, Tübingen, Germany

guardian style

launching it, whether intended or not. Effectively is almost invariably misused, and can often be omitted

effete does not mean effeminate or foppish, but "weak, ineffectual or decadent as a result of over-refinement ... exhausted, worn out, spent" (Collins)

efit (electronic facial identification technique) program used to create police drawings

eg no full point

EGM not egm; extraordinary general meeting

Eid al-Adha (Festival of Sacrifice) Muslim festival laid down in Islamic law, celebrates the end of the hajj. Note that eid means festival, so it is tautologous to describe it as the "Eid festival"

Eid al-Fitr Muslim festival of thanksgiving laid down in Islamic law, celebrates the end of Ramadan (al-fitr means the breaking of the fast)

eid mubarak not a festival but a greeting (mubarak means "may it be blessed")

Eire do not use; say Republic of Ireland or Irish Republic

elan no accent

ElBaradei, Mohamed director general of the International Atomic Energy Agency, ElBaradei after first mention

elderly do not use to describe anyone under 70, and say elderly people (or even better, older people), never "the elderly"

El Dorado fabled city of gold; **Eldorado** legendary flop of a soap

electra complex the female equivalent of oedipal complex

I discovered the Guardian stylebook while Googling to try to decide which of email or e-mail would win (a frightening number of web style guides blithely use both on the same page). What a wonderful find! Your stylebook is engaging, lucid and delightfully sensible.

**Andrew Ferguson,
Adelaide, Australia**

94

electrocution death by electric shock, so don't say survivors of torture were "electrocuted" during their ordeal – rather that they were given electric shocks

elegiac

elephant in the room

Our cliche of the year in 2006, when it appeared in the Guardian 38 times (twice as frequently as in 2005); elephants in the room – and sometimes, more precisely, in the living room – have included trade figures, policy, lack of policy, climate change, Iraq, the US, Europe, anti-Americanism, men, women, single women, a new French football league, race, religion, Islam, Catholicism, Tessa Jowell, Andrew Neil, Jimmy Greaves, fatness, thinness, Stalinism, Hitler and Tony Blair's departure from office.

Mercifully, this tedious expression already seems to be on its way to the elephant's graveyard

elite

ellipsis use spaces before and after ellipses, and three dots (with no spaces between them), eg "She didn't want to go there … "; there is no need for a full point

email

emanate is intransitive; use **exude** if you need a transitive verb

Embankment, the in London; the tube station is just **Embankment**

embargo plural **embargos**

embarrass, embarrassment

embassy lc, eg British embassy

emigrate leave a country; **immigrate** arrive in one

Emin, Tracey not Tracy

empathic not empathetic

empires lc British empire, Roman empire, etc

employment tribunal not industrial tribunal

EMS European monetary system

Emu economic and monetary union

enamoured of not by or with

enclose not inclose

encyclopedia not encyclopaedia

enervate to deprive of strength or vitality

enforce, enforceable

England, English take care not to offend readers from other parts of the UK by saying England or English when you mean Britain or British, and vice versa (we published a map of England's best beaches, with the headline "Britain's best beaches") *see Scotland*

English Heritage, English Partnerships

English Nature is now **Natural England**

en masse

enormity something monstrous or wicked; not synonymous with large

enquiry use **inquiry**

enrol, enrolling, enrolment

en route not on route

en suite two words, whatever estate agents might claim

ensure make certain; **insure** against risk; **assure** life

enthral, enthralling

entr'acte

E.ON UK parent of Powergen; **Eon** is our style for the German energy firm

epicentre the point on the earth's surface directly above the focus of an earthquake or underground explosion; frequently misused to mean the centre or focus itself

epilepsy we do not define people by their medical condition: seizures are epileptic, people are not; so say (if relevant) "Joe Bloggs, who has epilepsy ... " not "Joe Bloggs, an epileptic ... "

EPO erythropoietin, a performance-enhancing drug

equator, the

Equatorial Guinea formerly Spanish Guinea, a country in central Africa that became independent in 1974; do not confuse with Guinea or Guinea-Bissau, other African former colonies

ere long not e'er long

Eriksson, Sven-Göran

ERM exchange rate mechanism

Ernie electronic random number indicator equipment: the machine that picks winning premium bond numbers

escapers not escapees, despite the apparently unstoppable advance of the -ee suffix (can it be long before Guardian readers become "readees"?)

Eskimo is a language spoken in Greenland, Canada, Alaska and Siberia. Note that it has no more words for snow than English does for rain. The people are **Inuit** (singular **Inuk**), not "Eskimos"

espresso not expresso

establishment, the

estuary English

Eta Basque separatists; **ETA** estimated time of arrival

ethnic never say ethnic when you mean ethnic minority, which leads to such nonsense as "the constituency has a small ethnic population"

ethnic cleansing do not use as a euphemism for genocide unless in quotation marks

EU European Union (no need to spell out at first mention); formerly EC (European Community); before that EEC (European Economic Community)

EU presidents

There are three, so don't say "EU president" or "president of the union" without making clear which you mean: president of the European commission, president of the European parliament, or holder of the rotating presidency (technically "president in office of the council of the European Union"), which rotates among the member states every six months

euro currency; plural **euros** and **cents**

Euro do not use as a prefix to everything European, but **Euro-MP** is an acceptable alternative to MEP

Euro Disney runs what is now called Disneyland Paris

euroland, eurozone

Europe includes Britain, so don't say, for example, something is common "in Europe" unless it is common in Britain as well; to distinguish between Britain and the rest of Europe the phrase "continental Europe" may be useful; **central Europe**, **eastern Europe**, **western Europe**

European commission the commission after first mention; do not abbreviate to EC

European convention on human rights

European court of human rights nothing to do with the EU: it is a Council of Europe body

Eurosceptic one word, capped: they are sceptics about the EU, not just the euro

Eurovision song contest

evangelical fundamentalist wing of Christianity

evangelist someone who spreads the gospel

eventually as in "the FTSE 100 drifted back, eventually closing 33.9 points lower at 5244.2"; the stockmarket always closes eventually so you don't need it here or in most other places it crops up

every day noun and adverb: it happens every day; **everyday** adjective: an everyday mistake

every parent's nightmare avoid this cliché

I do think that you need, as a paper, to correct the overuse of the term "every parent's nightmare". It seems to crop up for anything to do with children, from abduction to serious death to today's piece on musical taste. As a parent, I can't cope with that many nightmares.

**Stuart Haynes,
Liverpool**

exchequer, the

exclamation marks do not use!

exclusive term used by tabloid newspapers to denote a story that is in all of them

execution the carrying out of a death sentence by lawful authority, so a terrorist, for example, does not "execute" someone

ex officio by right of position or office

ex parte on behalf of one party only

expat, expatriate not ex-pat or expatriot; this is "ex" meaning "out of" (as in export, extract), not "ex-" meaning "former" (as in ex-husband)

explained "said" is normally sufficient

Export Credits Guarantee Department ECGD at second mention

exposé

extracurricular, extramarital, extraterrestrial, extraterritorial

extrovert not extravert

eye level no hyphen

eyes is being used increasingly for "considers", but it doesn't mean that so don't use it in this way. You might get away with "BoS eyes up Abbey" meaning considers it as a takeover target, but not "BoS eyes online insurance" meaning BoS considers setting up an online sales operation

eyewitness one word, but **witness** is preferable, except in the Guardian's Eyewitness picture spread

Ff

"Say all you have to say in the fewest possible words, or your reader will be sure to skip them; and in the plainest possible words, or he will certainly misunderstand them."

John Ruskin

facade no cedilla

facelift

factchecker, factchecking

factoid not a trivial fact, but a mistaken assumption repeated so often that it is believed to be true (a word coined by Norman Mailer, who defined it as "something that everyone knows is true, except it ain't!")

FA Cup the Cup (the cap C is hallowed by convention); all other cups lc at second mention

fahrenheit use in brackets, without degree symbol, after celsius figure, eg 37C (98.6F); to convert, multiply the celsius temperature by 1.8, then add 32; alternatively, double the celsius figure, subtract one-tenth of that figure, and add 32; or you could save yourself the bother by using a conversion website

Fáilte Ireland Ireland's tourism authority

Fairtrade The Fairtrade mark is a certification system run by the Fairtrade Foundation; products are entitled to be called Fairtrade (cap F) if they meet the following criteria: a price that covers producers' costs, a premium for producers to invest in their communities, and long-term and more direct trading relations; **fair trade** refers to the movement as a whole, eg only fair trade will enable farmers in developing countries to become self-sufficient

fairytale noun and adjective

falafel

fallopian tubes

fallout

family-size, fun-size not family-sized, fun-sized

famous, famously overused and often unnecessary

fanbelt, fanclub, fanmail

far, farther, farthest of distances, otherwise **further, furthest**

far away adverb **faraway** adjective; she moved to a faraway place, and now lives far away

far east but **east Asia** or **south-east Asia** is preferable

farm worker not farm labourer

Faroe Isles or just **Faroes**

farrago a hotchpotch or jumbled mixture, not synonymous with fiasco (a humiliating failure)

Farsi language spoken by the majority of Iranians (not Persian)

fascism, fascist not facism, facist, a careless but common error

fashion weeks lc, eg London fashion week

fatality use death

fat cats use sparingly, unless writing about overweight moggies

father of two, mother of two, etc (no hyphens); only describe people in this way if relevant

Father's Day

fatwa an edict, not necessarily a death sentence

fayre say **fair**

fazed overwhelmed; **phased** staged

FBI Federal Bureau of Investigation; no need to spell out

FDA what the former First Division Association now calls itself; you will need to say it is the senior civil servants' union or no one will know who you are talking about; note that FDA also stands for the US food and drug administration

fedayeen Arab fighters (the word means those who risk their lives for a cause); can be capped up when referring to a specific force, eg the Saddam Fedayeen militia, which fought coalition forces in the 2003 Iraq war

Federal Reserve at first reference, **the Fed** thereafter

fed up with not fed up of

feelgood factor

fellow lc, eg a fellow of All Souls, fellow artist, fellow members, etc (and do not hyphenate)

female not "woman" or "women" in such phrases as female home secretary, female voters

female genital mutilation not "female circumcision"

ferris wheel do not cap up

festivals lc, whether artistic or sporting: Cannes film festival, Cheltenham festival, Edinburgh Fringe festival, Reading festival, etc

fete no accent

fewer or **less**? fewer means smaller in number, eg fewer coins; less means smaller in quantity, eg less money

I have just printed out the Guardian style guide and am thrilled by all the useful and funny things I'm reading. Thank you for correctly pointing out that Finland is not part of Scandinavia. I'd already given up on trying to convince people – English AND Finnish!

**Annika Akerfelt,
Oldenburg, Germany**

Ffestiniog

fiance male, **fiancee** female; but note divorcee is both male and female

Fianna Fáil Irish political party

fiasco like debacle and farce, overused in news stories: who says it's a fiasco?

field marshal

figures spell out from one to nine; numerals from 10 to 999,999; thereafter 1m, 3.2bn (except for people and animals, eg 2 million viewers, 8 billion cattle)

filesharing

fillip not filip

film-maker but **film star**

Filofax TM; use **personal organiser** unless you are sure

finalise, finalised avoid, use **complete, completed** or **finish, finished**

Financial Services Authority FSA on second mention

financial years 2004-05, etc

Fine Gael Irish political party

fine-tooth comb

Finnegans Wake

firebomb

fire brigade, fire service lc, eg Cheshire fire brigade

firefight do not use to describe a military skirmish

firefighter not fireman

firing line the people who do the firing; if they are aiming at you, you are **in the line of fire** not in the firing line

firm strictly a partnership without limited liability, such as solicitors or accountants, but may be used in place of company in headlines

first, second, third rather than firstly, secondly, thirdly, etc; spell out up to ninth, then 10th, 21st, millionth

first aid

first-hand

first lady

first minister (Scottish parliament, Welsh assembly, Northern Ireland assembly)

first name, forename, given name not Christian name

first world war

fit for purpose a recent cliche that quickly proved itself unfit for the purpose of good writing

fit the bill not fill the bill

flagship a flagship is a ship, a "flagship store" would be a store where one bought flagships, and a "flagship local authority" is a cliche

flak not flack

flammable rather than inflammable (although, curiously, they mean the same thing); the negative is **non-flammable**

flash memory computer memory that can be erased and reprogrammed, used for example in mobile phones, digital cameras and MP3 players

flatmate

flaunt or **flout**? to flaunt is to make a display of something, as in flaunting wealth; to flout is to show disregard for something, as in flouting the seatbelt law

fledgling not fledgeling

flexitime

flotation whether in a tank, or on the stockmarket

flounder or **founder**? to flounder is to perform a task badly, like someone stuck in mud; to founder is to fail: a business might be foundering because its bosses are floundering

flu

fluky not flukey

flyer not flier

flying squad

flypast noun

fo'c'sle abbreviation of forecastle

focus, focused, focusing

foetid not fetid

foetus not fetus

fogey not fogy

folklore, folksong

following prefer after, eg Leeds United went to pieces after yet another relegation

font (typeface) not fount

foolproof

foot-and-mouth disease

footie abbreviation for football, but note that in Australia (particularly Victoria), **footy** is what they call Australian rules football

for all its worth but **for what it's worth**

forbear abstain; **forebear** ancestor

foreign accents

Use accents on French, German, Spanish, and Irish Gaelic words – and, if at all possible, on people's names in any language, eg Sven-Göran Erikkson (Swedish), José Manuel Barroso (Portuguese). This may be tricky in the case of some languages but we have had complaints from readers that it is disrespectful to foreign readers to, in effect, misspell their names

Foreign Office abbreviate to FCO not FO as its official name is Foreign and Commonwealth Office

foreign placenames

Style for foreign placenames evolves with common usage. Leghorn
has become Livorno, and maybe one day München will supplant
Munich, but not yet. Remember that many names have become part
of the English language: Geneva is the English name for the city that
Switzerland's French speakers refer to as Genève and its German
speakers call Genf.

Accordingly, we opt for locally used names, with these main
exceptions (the list is not exhaustive, apply common sense):
Archangel, Basle, Berne, Brittany, Cologne, Dunkirk, Florence,
Fribourg, Genoa, Gothenburg, Hanover, Kiev, Lombardy, Milan,
Munich, Naples, Normandy, Nuremberg, Padua, Piedmont, Rome,
Sardinia, Seville, Sicily, Syracuse, Turin, Tuscany, Venice, Zurich.

And the next time someone says we should call Burma
"Myanmar" because that's what it calls itself, point out that Colonel
Gadafy renamed Libya "The Great Socialist People's Libyan Arab
Jamahiriyya"

foreign secretary

foreign words and phrases

Italicise, with roman translation in brackets, if it really is a foreign
word or phrase and not an anglicised one, in which case it is roman
with no accents (exceptions: exposé, pâté, résumé, roué).

Remember Orwell: do not use a foreign word where a suitable
English equivalent exists

forensic belonging to the courts; does not mean scientific

foresee, foreseeable

Forestry Commission

forever continually: he is forever changing his mind; **for ever** for always: I will love you for ever

forgo go without; **forego** go before

forklift truck

former Soviet republics

These are:

Armenia adjective **Armenian**

Azerbaijan adjective **Azerbaijani** (though there are ethnic Azeris in, eg, Armenia)

Belarus adjective **Belarussian**

Estonia adjective **Estonian** (Estonia did not join the Commonwealth of Independent States)

Georgia adjective **Georgian**

Kazakhstan adjective **Kazakh**

Kyrgyzstan adjective **Kyrgyz**

Latvia adjective **Latvian** (not in the commonwealth)

Lithuania adjective **Lithuanian** (not in the commonwealth)

Moldova adjective **Moldovan**

Russia adjective **Russian**

Tajikistan adjective **Tajik**

Turkmenistan adjective **Turkmen** (its citizens are Turkmen, singular Turkman)

Ukraine adjective **Ukrainian** (not "the Ukraine")

Uzbekistan adjective **Uzbek**

Formica TM

formula plural **formulas**, but **formulae** in scientific context

formula one motor racing

fortuitous by chance, not (as most people seem to think) by good fortune; if we manage to use the word correctly, it is entirely fortuitous

fosbury flop

Fourth of July

foxhunting

FPA Family Planning Association at first mention, thereafter the FPA, although the organisation has decided to style itself "fpa" (lc, no definite article) in its literature and on its website

FRA fellow of the Royal Academy; **FRS** fellow of the Royal Society

fractions two-thirds, three-quarters, etc, but two and a half, but use ⅓, ¾ in tables, recipes, etc

Frankenstein the monster's creator, not the monster

Frankenstein food has become a cliche to describe GM food; do not use

fraud squad

free or **for nothing** are preferable to "for free"

freefall

french fries, french horn, french kiss, french letter, french polish, french window

French Guiana an overseas *département* of France on the Caribbean coast of South America; do not confuse with Equatorial Guinea, Guinea, or Guinea-Bissau, which are all in Africa, or Guyana, which is also in South America

fresco plural **frescoes**

Freud, Lucian British artist, not Lucien

freudian slip

friendlily curious adverb defined by the OED as "in a friendly manner, like a friend"

friendly fire no quotation marks necessary

Friends of the Earth abbreviate to FoE after first mention

Friends Provident no apostrophe

Frisbee TM; if in doubt, call it a flying disc

frontbench, frontline, frontman, frontrunner

frostbite, frostbitten

FTSE 100

fuck do not describe this as "a good, honest old-fashioned Anglo-Saxon word" because, first, there is no such thing as an Anglo-Saxon word (they spoke Old English) and, more important, its first recorded use dates from 1278 *see swearwords*

fuel overused as a verb

Fulbright scholarship not Fullbright

fulfil, fulfilling, fulfilment

full-time

fulsome another example of a word that is almost never used correctly, it means "cloying, excessive, disgusting by excess" (and is not, as some appear to believe, a clever word for full); so "fulsome praise" should not be used in a complimentary sense

fundraiser, fundraising

fungus plural **fungi**

Why don't your subeditors bother to check before using foreign words and phrases they clearly aren't familiar with? Do they think they are somehow above this or that foreign phrases don't need to be spelled correctly? It's so depressing, from a newspaper that claims to be international, sophisticated, etc. Latest offender: "Room mit ein view" ... My German husband groaned and said he is never going to read the paper again.

Jo Griffin, London

Gg

"I have made this letter longer
only because I have not had the
time to make it shorter."

Blaise Pascal

Gg

G8 Canada, France, Germany, Italy, Japan, the United Kingdom, the United States and the newest member, Russia

Gadafy, Muammar Libyan leader rather than president (he holds no government office and is generally known in Libya as "leader of the revolution"); Gadafy on second mention

gaff hook or spar, also slang for house; **blow the gaff** give away a secret; **gaffe** blunder

Galápagos

Gallagher Oasis brothers (Noel and Liam); **Gallaher** cigarette company

Gambia, the not Gambia

gambit an opening strategy that involves some sacrifice or concession; so to talk of an opening gambit is tautologous – an opening ploy might be better

Game Boy

gameplan, gameshow

Gandhi not Ghandi

García Lorca, Federico (1898-1936) Spanish writer

García Márquez, Gabriel Colombian novelist

Garda Síochána Irish police force; **garda** (plural **gardaí**) police officer

garotte not garrotte or garrote

garryowen up-and-under (rugby union); **Garryowen** Irish rugby club

gases plural of gas, but the verb is **gasses**

Gatt general agreement on tariffs and trade

Gaudí, Antoni (1852-1926) Catalan architect

Gauguin, Paul (1848-1903) French painter

gay use as an adjective rather than a noun: a gay man, gay people, gay men and lesbians not "gays and lesbians"

Gaza Strip

Gb gigabits; **GB** gigabytes

GCSE A* not A-star

gender issues

Our use of language reflects Guardian values, as well changes in society. Phrases such as career girl or career woman, for example, are outdated (more women have careers than men) and patronising (there is no male equivalent): never use them.

actor, comedian: covers men and women; not actress, comedienne (but **waiter** and **waitress** are acceptable – at least for the moment).

firefighter, not fireman; **PC**, not WPC (police forces have abandoned the distinction), **postal workers,** not postmen.

Avoid terms such as businessmen, housewives, male nurse, woman pilot, woman (lady!) doctor, etc, which reinforce outdated stereotypes. If you need to use an adjective, it is **female** and not "woman" in such phrases as female MPs, female president.

Use **humankind** or **humanity** rather than mankind, a word that, as one of our readers points out, "alienates half the population from their own history".

Never say "his" to cover men and women: use his or her, or a different construction; in sentences such as "a teacher who beats

I know that it's sensible and polite to use gender-neutral nouns such as firefighter and police officer, but what about the people who deliver the post?
Alan Cox, Edinburgh

his/her pupils is not fit to do the job", there is usually a way round the problem – in this case, "teachers who beat their pupils ... "

Men who occasionally question our robust policy and accuse the Guardian of "political correctness" may care to reflect on the fact that Fowler's used to list such "established feminine titles" as adventuress, authoress, doctress, editress, inspectress, executrix, giantess, huntress, Jewess, poetess, procuress, quakeress, songstress, tailoress, wardress; it also recommended using new ones such as danceress and teacheress, pointing out that "with the coming extension of women's vocations, feminines for vocation-words are a special need of the future; everyone knows the inconvenience of being uncertain whether a doctor is a man or a woman ... "

It seems ironic that the term "gays" appears so liberally in a Guardian article championing the equality of homosexuals. Can we please get one thing straight. We are gay *people*.
Emma Sherrington,
London

general General Tommy Franks at first mention, then Franks

general election

General Medical Council (GMC), doctors' disciplinary body

General Strike (1926)

Geneva conventions (not convention); four treaties, last revised and ratified in 1949, which with three more recently adopted protocols set out international standards for the humanitarian treatment of prisoners of war and civilians caught up in war

geography distinct areas are capped up: Black Country, East Anglia, Lake District, Midlands, Peak District, West Country; but areas defined by compass points are lc: the north, the south-east, the south-west, etc

geordie noun and adjective; refers to people from Tyneside, and their accent

geriatrics branch of medicine dealing with elderly people, not an amusing way to describe them in an attempt to make yourself sound cool

german measles but rubella is preferable

ghetto plural **ghettoes**

ghoti George Bernard Shaw's proposed spelling of the word "fish" (gh as in trough, o as in women, ti as in nation)

giant We know that BP and Vodafone are big companies, so don't need to be told that they are "the telecoms giant" or "the oil giant"

giantkiller, giantkilling no hyphen

Gibraltar overseas territory or dependency, not a British colony; its inhabitants are **Gibraltarians**

gift not a verb (unless, perhaps, directly quoting a football manager or player: "We gifted Spurs their second goal")

girl female under 18

girlfriend

girlie noun (only when quoting someone); **girly** adjective (eg girly clothes); **girlish** behaviour

Giscard d'Estaing, Valéry former French president, Giscard on second mention

Giuliani, Rudolph or **Rudy** (not Rudi) former New York mayor

Giuseppe regularly misspelt as Guiseppe; this is sloppy

Gg

GLA

A mistake we repeat ad nauseam is the assumption that GLA stands for "Greater London assembly". There is no such thing. The **Greater London authority** comprises the mayor, who runs it, and the **London assembly**, which holds the mayor to account

glamorous not glamourous

Glasgow kiss a head-butt

glasnost

GlaxoSmithKline GSK on second mention and in headlines

GM crops, GM food no need to write genetically modified in full at first mention

GMT Greenwich mean time: the ship ran aground at 8am local time (0700 GMT)

goalline, goalpost

goat's cheese

gobbledegook

gobsmacked use only when directly quoting someone

God

godchild, godfather, godmother, godparents, godson, goddaughter

Goldsmiths College no apostrophe

golf for holes, use numbers: 1st, 2nd, 18th, etc; matchplay: one word, except World Match Play Championship; the Open, not the British Open

Good Friday agreement

goodness, for goodness sake

goodnight

Google cap up, even when used as a verb ("I Googled myself"); named after googol, the number 1 followed by 100 zeros or 10^{100}

Gormley, Antony

go-slow noun; **go slow** verb

Goths (uc) Germanic tribe that invaded the Roman empire

goths (lc) Sisters of Mercy fans who invaded the Shepherd's Bush Empire

government lc in all contexts and all countries; resist the awful trend to say such things as "Lord Browne fended off accusations of being too close to government" – it should be **the government**

government departments *see departments of state*

graffiti are plural; **graffito** is the singular

grammar the set of rules followed by speakers of a language, rather than a set of arbitrary dos and don'ts, or as Ambrose Bierce put it, "a system of pitfalls thoughtfully prepared for the feet of the self-made man"

Grammer, Kelsey

grandad but **granddaughter**

grandparent

Mention this status only when relevant: leave "battling grannies" and similar examples of ageism and sexism to the tabloids; in particular we should avoid such patronising drivel as "How this 55-year-old granny came to earn $25m a year" (page 1 blurb) – just in case anyone still didn't get the message, the front of G2 said: "She's five foot two, she's a grandmother and she earns $25m a year"

grand prix plural **grands prix**

grassroots one word

great-aunt, great-grandfather, great-great-grandmother, etc

Great Britain England, Wales and Scotland; if you want to include Northern Ireland, use Britain or the UK

green a green activist, the green movement, but uc when referring to so-named political parties, eg the German Greens

green belt designated areas around cities subject to strict planning controls, not open countryside in general

greenfield site one that has not been built on before; one that has been built on before is a **brownfield site**

greengrocer's apostrophe *see apostrophes*

> Why is Lindis Percy the peace campaigner ("Anti-war protester escapes asbo") described as a "Yorkshire grandmother"? What bearing does the fertility of her children have on the story? Would a man in her position have been defined as a grandfather?
> **Lindy Hardcastle, Groby, Leicestershire**

greenhouse effect

Energy from the Earth's surface is trapped in the lower atmosphere
by gases that prevent it leaking into space, a natural phenomenon
that makes life possible, whose enhancement by natural or artificial
means may make life impossible. Not the result of the hole in the
ozone layer, whose thinning in the upper atmosphere is due to CFCs;
the connection is that CFCs are also greenhouse gases

green paper

grisly gruesome; **grizzly** bear

Grossman, Loyd TV presenter and chef with his own brand of
pasta sauces, former singer with Jet Bronx and the Forbidden

Ground Zero caps for former site of World Trade Centre in New
York, lc for referring to the exact location of explosions, eg at
Hiroshima in 1945

grow an intransitive verb, so flowers may grow but companies
don't "grow profits" and governments don't "grow economies"

Guantánamo Bay

guerrilla

Guevara, Che (1928-67) Argentine-born revolutionary

Guggenheim Museum cap M if you use the word, although it
is not normally necessary. Frank Lloyd Wright designed the
Guggenheim in New York, Frank Gehry the one in Bilbao (and
another proposed for Abu Dhabi). We have sometimes confused
the two

Guides not "Girl Guides"; the organisation is Girlguiding UK

Guildhall (City of London), not "the Guildhall"

Guinea formerly French Guinea, a republic in north-west Africa that became independent in 1958; do not confuse with Equatorial Guinea, French Guiana, Guinea-Bissau, or Guyana

Guinea-Bissau formerly Portuguese Guinea, independent since 1974, lying on the coast to the north-west of Guinea

guineapig

guineas younger readers may not be aware that a guinea was worth £1 1s (£1.05) unless they buy or sell racehorses (the buyer still pays the auction house in guineas, and the auction house then gives the vendor the same number of pounds, thus netting the auctioneer his 5% commission)

Gulf, the not the Persian or Arabian Gulf

Gulf war of 1991

gun battle not gunbattle, and not "firefight"

Gurkha

GUS the former Great Universal Stores split into the credit rating agency Experian and Home Retail Group in 2006

guttural not gutteral

Guyana formerly British Guiana, a nation in South America that gained its independence in 1812; not to be confused with French Guiana or the three African states of Equatorial Guinea, Guinea, and Guinea-Bissau; its inhabitants are Guyanese (noun and adjective), not Guyanan

Gypsies recognised as an ethnic group under the Race Relations Act, as are Irish Travellers, hence capped up

Hh

"Would you convey my compliments to the purist who reads your proofs and tell him or her that I write in a sort of broken-down patois which is something like the way a Swiss waiter talks, and that when I split an infinitive, God damn it, I split it so it will stay split."

Raymond Chandler

Häagen-Dazs American ice-cream; despite appearances, the name was made up to give a European cachet to a product emanating from the Bronx in New York City

Ha'aretz Israeli newspaper

Haarlem the Netherlands; **Harlem** New York City

habeas corpus

Haberdashers' Aske's school

Habsburg not Hapsburg

haemorrhaging is best avoided, even if you manage to spell it correctly, as it has become a cliche – in expressions such as "haemorrhaging cash" – and completely wrong as an adjective meaning big, eg "in the face of haemorrhaging financial losses"

haemorrhoids

Hague, The always cap up "The"

Hair, Darrell Australian umpire who officiated at the abandoned Test between England and Pakistan at the Oval in 2006

hairbrush, haircut, hairdresser, hairdryer, hairstyle all one word

Haiti is not an island: Haiti and the Dominican Republic make up the Caribbean island of Hispaniola

hajj pilgrimage to Mecca; a Muslim who has made such a pilgrimage is a **haji**

haka Maori war dance, as performed by the New Zealand All Blacks rugby team

Hale-Bopp comet its appearance in 1997 prompted mass suicide in the Heaven's Gate cult

half no hyphen when used adverbially: you look half dead; half wine, half water; his trousers were at half mast; the scores were level at half time.

hyphen when used adjectivally: a half-eaten sandwich; a half-cut subeditor; half-hearted Hannah; half-time oranges.

The boy is six and a half; a six and a half-year-old boy

half a dozen, half past six

half-life (radioactivity)

halfway, halfwit

Hallé orchestra founded in Manchester by Karl Hallé in 1857

Halley's comet

Halloween

halo plural **haloes**

Hambros bank

Hamed, Prince Naseem former boxer; Hamed at second mention

Hamilton Academical not Academicals, nickname the Accies

Hamleys

handbill, handbook, handbuilt, handheld, handmade, handout no hyphens

handicapped do not use to refer to people with disabilities or learning difficulties

hangar aircraft; **hanger** clothes

hanging participles

An unfortunate example from a leading article in the paper: "Due out in January as a white paper, Ms Kelly may be unable to overcome Mr Blair's apparent determination to stick with A-levels ... " *see dangling participles*

Hanover

Hanukah

happy-clappy avoid

hara-kiri known less vulgarly in Japan as **seppuku**

harass, harassment

hardcore one word, whether noun or adjective and whether you are talking about music, rubble, a hardcore of rebels or hardcore pornography

hardline adjective; **hard line**, **hardliner** nouns

harebrained not hairbrained

hare lip never use: say **cleft lip** or **cleft palate**

Haringey north London borough, one ward of which is **Harringay**

Hariri, Rafik former prime minister of Lebanon, assassinated in Beirut in 2005

Harley-Davidson

HarperCollins

Harper's Bazaar US fashion magazine marketed as **Harper's Bazaar UK** in Britain, where it was known as Harpers & Queen from 1970 to 2006

Harpers Bizarre 60s US harmony group and exponents of "cotton candy rock", named after the magazine

Harrods

Hassidic

hat-trick

Haverfordwest in south-west Wales, not "Haverford West" as we managed to say

Havisham, Miss (not Haversham) in Dickens' Great Expectations

Hawaiian

Hawk-Eye (not Hawkeye) tracks the ball in cricket and tennis

Hay the **Guardian Hay festival** takes place at **Hay-on-Wye**

hay fever

hazard or risk?

Scientists use hazard to mean a potential for harm and risk to mean the actual probability of harm occurring; though headline writers may feel more at home with risk than hazard, the distinction is worth bearing in mind

guardian style

HBOS (not HBoS) created in 2001 by the merger of Halifax and Bank of Scotland

HD DVD

head-butt (but **butt** should normally suffice)

headdress, headhunter, headroom but **head-on**

headquarters can be used as a singular ("a large headquarters") or plural ("our headquarters are in London"); HQ, however, takes the singular

headteacher one word, not headmaster, headmistress; but **Association of Head Teachers**

Health and Safety Executive HSE on second mention

healthcare

hear, hear

exclamation of approval that we have misspelt as "here, here" on more than one occasion

heartbroken, heartfelt, heartsearching, heartwarming but **heart-rending, heart-throb**

Heart of Midlothian Edinburgh football club commonly known as **Hearts**; said to be named after a dancehall that in turn took its name from Sir Walter Scott's 1818 novel The Heart of Midlothian

Heathrow airport or simply **Heathrow**; not "London's Heathrow"

heatwave

heaven

hectares convert to acres in brackets at first mention by multiplying by 2.47, so 10 hectares is 24.7 acres; to convert acres to hectares, multiply by 0.4, so 10 acres is 4 hectares (we get this the wrong way round embarrassingly often)

height in metres with imperial conversion, eg 1.68 metres (5ft 7in)

heir apparent someone certain to inherit from a deceased unless he or she dies first or is taken out of the will; don't use to mean "likely successor"

hell, hades

hello not hallo (and certainly not "hullo", unless quoting the Rev ARP Blair)

Hells Angels no apostrophe

help help to decide or help decide; not "help and decide"

helpline

hemisphere northern hemisphere, southern hemisphere

herculean

here generally avoid if what you mean is "in Britain"

Hergé pen name of Georges Remi (1907-83), Belgian creator of Tintin

Heritage Lottery Fund

Hermès scarf people; **Hermes Group** fund manager

Headlines

What makes a great, or at least memorable, headline? They can be historic ("Man walks on Moon"), campaigning ("A liar and a cheat"), classical ("Between Cilla and Charybdis"), subtle ("Flo quiets the Dons"), funny ("Super Caley go ballistic – Celtic are atrocious"), notorious ("Gotcha!"), or downright absurd ("Freddie Starr ate my hamster"). There is no magic formula but here are a few guidelines.

Use active verbs where possible, particularly in news headlines: "Editor updates style guidelines" is much better than "Style guidelines updated". Avoid tabloid cliches such as bid, brand, dub and slam, and their broadsheet counterparts such as insist, signal and target. Imagining that you are describing an event, in words, to real people, is a good antidote to journalese: no one in a pub says "Did you see that Brown slammed Blair in a dramatic power bid?"

Just as we would in copy, we need to take care with words such as debacle, farce and fiasco, especially when combined, which we contrived to do in the headline "Hips fiasco descends into farce" – the fact that "Hips farce descends into fiasco" would work just as well tells you something is probably wrong here.

Strive to be fresh: tired plays on the phrase "Mind the gap", heard only occasionally these days by passengers on the London underground, have become tedious, as well as either baffling or infuriating to readers who do not happen to live in the capital.

Take care over ambiguity: "Landmine claims dog UK arms firm", which appeared in the paper, contains so many successive nouns, some of which may or may not be verbs, that you have to read it several times to work out what it means.

Exclamation marks – look, I've written something funny! – should never be used. Question marks are also to be avoided, as are quotation marks, unless essential to signify a quote or for legal reasons. And we should resist the temptation to save space by replacing "and" with a comma: "Blair and Brown agree euro deal" not "Blair, Brown agree euro deal".

Puns are fine – "Where there's muck there's bras", about a farmer's wife who started a lingerie business from a barn, was voted headline of the year by our staff – but do not overuse, or resort to tired puns such as "flushed with success" (this story has got a plumber in it). It is possible to try just a little too hard ("To baldly grow where no mane's grown before"). In the 1970s and 80s the Guardian suffered from a reputation for excruciating puns; today, we want to be known for clever, original and witty headlines.

Unexpected twists, or subtle plays on words and phrases, show the subeditor's craft at its best: a power failure in a theatre became, in the Guardian, "Bad lights stop play". A light touch can work beautifully: "Drop dead, gorgeous", on a story about office jealousy, added one comma to a well-known film title to create the perfect headline. When Tate Modern exhibited a giant sun, to create its own indoor climate, the beautiful headline written by the Guardian's Steve Chamberlain – "But is it weather?" (a rare example of a question mark being required) – deserved to be framed and exhibited in a gallery in its own right.

Be careful when making references to popular culture: "Mrs Culpepper's lonely hearts club banned" works, because most people are familiar with the Beatles' Sgt Pepper album, but allusions to your favourite obscure prog-rock LP are likely to pass over most readers' heads. Long after most people had forgotten the 1960s movie Charlie Bubbles, tabloid sports subeditors continued to mystify their readers by using the headline "Charlie bubbles" whenever anyone called Charlie scored a goal. "Book lack in Ongar", about a shortage of resources in Essex libraries, remains one of the all-time great headlines, but it only works if you get the reference to John Osborne's 1956 play Look Back in Anger (or at least it did until Oasis helpfully recorded a song called Don't Look Back in Anger).

It's time for some formulaic headlines to be given a decent burial, or at least a long rest. "The kids are alright" (based on a song by the Who, and subsequently a film) crops up, with minor variations, on a weekly and sometimes daily basis in British newspapers: "The kids are alright online", "The kids are all right (and left)", "The kids are all right, left and centre", and so on.

Even more ubiquitous are "Size isn't everything" and its close relative "Size doesn't matter", used to refer to a car (in two different newspapers), school uniforms, the actor Simon Callow's height, a hotel in Turkey, new houses, national economies, motorbikes, a footballer, the gallery following a golf tournament, and – once – penis size.

> The most important thing is to think of the readers and remember that we are writing headlines for their benefit

The ever-popular "Brighton rocks" and its variations are an allusion, still common, to the Graham Greene novel and subsequent film, both more than 50 years old. How many people still understand the reference? "So lucky, lucky, lucky", a recent headline we used above a photograph of Kylie Minogue, quoted lyrics from a hit she had in nearly 20 years ago. How many of our readers would be aware of this? You have to use your judgment.

If you are quoting, be sure to get it right. "Talkin' about their generation", from a classic 1960s song by the Who, fails as a headline because it literally lacks rhythm (it should be "Talkin' 'bout"). We claimed that Millwall fans sing "No one likes us and we don't care"; they don't sing that, and the mistake made it look as if we don't care.

As always, the most important thing is to think of the readers and remember that we are writing headlines for their benefit, not for our own amusement or to show how clever we are.

Hewlett-Packard or **HP**

Hibernian Edinburgh football club commonly known as **Hibs**

hiccup not hiccough

hi-fi how we listened to music in the days before iPods (short for high fidelity)

highchair

high commissioner sent from one Commonwealth country to another (rather than an ambassador)

high court

highfalutin

high flyer noun; **high-flying** adjective

highland fling

Highlands, the (Scotland)

high street lc in retail spending stories: "the recession is making an impact in the high street"; capped only in the proper name: "I went shopping in Walthamstow High Street"

Highways Agency

hijab covering for the head and face worn by some Muslim women

hijack of movable objects only, not of schools, embassies, etc

hike a walk, not an increase in interest rates; "Motorists face new petrol hike" (not one of our better headlines) suggested a long walk to a garage rather than simply a price rise

Hindi language; **Hindu** religion

Hip home information pack

hip-hop

hippopotamus plural **hippopotamuses**

hippy plural **hippies**

Hirst, Damien

His Master's Voice TM (picture of Nipper the dog with phonograph)

historian, historic use a not an, unless in a direct quote

HIT Entertainment

hitchhiker, hitchhiking no hyphens

hi-tech

HIV a virus, not a disease, but do not call HIV "the Aids virus" or an HIV test an "Aids test"; an HIV-positive man (hyphen) is HIV positive (no hyphen)

Hizbullah not Hezbollah; it means "party of God"

HM or **Her Majesty** for the Queen, not HRH

HMS Her Majesty's Ship: does not need the definite article, so it is "HMS Pinafore" rather than "the HMS Pinafore"

hoard or **horde**? a hoard of treasure; a horde (or hordes) of tourists

Hobson's choice a "choice" between taking what is offered and nothing at all

Ho Chi Minh City formerly Saigon

Hoddle, Glenn

hoi polloi common people, the masses; "the hoi polloi" is acceptable, even for speakers of ancient Greek

holidaymaker

Holland do not use when you mean the Netherlands (of which it is a region), with the exception of the Dutch football team, who are conventionally known as Holland

Holocaust do not trivialise by comparing piles of cattle during the foot-and-mouth outbreak to the Holocaust, or through phrases such as "Belsen-skinny" which, incredibly, found its way into a story about Kate Winslet

holy communion

holy grail

Holy Land

Holyrood home of Scotland's parliament, in Edinburgh

Holyroodhouse the Queen's official residence in Scotland

homebuyer, homeowner

home counties

home in not hone in

homeland but **home town**

homemade

Home Office but **home secretary** (although the official title is "Secretary of State for the Home Department")

homeopathy

homeowner, homepage

homogeneous uniform, of the same kind **homogenous** (biology) having a common descent; the latter is often misused for the former

homosexual rape do not use; say rape (or male rape if necessary)

honeybee

Hong Kong names like Taiwanese and Korean names, Hong Kong names are written in two parts with a hyphen, eg Tung Chee-hwa (Tung after first mention)

hon members of parliament

honorarium plural **honorariums**

honorary knights are not given titles, so it is still plain "Geldof" rather than "Sir Bob"

honorifics

Use just the surname after first mention, except in leading articles. This means that news stories, in the paper and on the web, now follow the style adopted by features and sport several years ago.

So: Gordon Brown at first mention, thereafter Brown; Harriet Harman at first mention, subsequently Harman; Sir Richard Branson at first mention, thereafter Branson; Lord Adonis at first mention, subsequently Adonis; Prof John Wells, at first mention, thereafter Wells; Dr Bill Bailey (and all other medical and scientific doctors and doctors of divinity) at first mention, subsequently Bailey; the Rev Clifford Richard at first mention, thereafter Richard, etc.

As always, use common sense: in a story where two people have the same name (eg a court case about a husband and wife or a story involving brothers), it may be necessary to use Mr and Mrs or Ms, or forenames.

Follow traditional Guardian style in leading articles (but not in other comment pieces and columns on leader pages): use honorifics after first mention, unless writing about an artist, author, journalist, sportsman or woman, musician, criminal or dead person; use Ms for women on second mention unless they have expressed a preference for Miss or Mrs.

So: at first mention Gordon Brown, Harriet Harman, Sir Richard Branson, Lord Adonis, Prof John Wells, Dr Bill Bailey, the Rev Clifford Richard; thereafter Mr Brown, Ms Harman, Sir Richard, Lord Adonis, Prof Wells, Dr Bailey, Mr Richard, etc

"honour" killings always use quotes; as a reader says: "There is no honour involved in these murders and calling them honour killings belittles the victims and plays down the crime"

hoodie a hooded top, as well as someone who wears one

Hoover TM; say **vacuum cleaner** unless you are sure it is a Hoover (uc); but lc for figurative **hoovering up** (eg "the Guardian website hoovered up all the awards")

hopefully like many other adverbs, such as frankly, happily, honestly and sadly, hopefully can be used as a "sentence adverb" indicating the writer's view of events – "hopefully, we will reach the summit" – or as a "manner adverb" modifying a verb – "we set off hopefully for the summit". Why some people are upset by "hopefully we will win" and not "sadly we lost" is a mystery

horrendous sounds like a rather ugly combination of horrific and tremendous, but is in fact from the Latin for fearful; **horrific** is generally preferable

horticulturist not horticulturalist

hospitalised do not use; say someone was taken (never "rushed") to hospital

hospitals cap the placename, eg Derby district general hospital, Great Ormond Street children's hospital, Royal London hospital

hotdog

hotels a hotel not "an"; do not cap up "hotel": the Dorchester, the Ritz, the Grand hotel, Brighton, etc (but don't be daft and lower-case Hotel California)

hotline, hotspot

hot-water bottle

houseboat, housebreaker, housebuyer, householder, housekeeper, housemate

househusband, housewife use with care; avoid sexist stereotyping such as lower food prices being "good news for housewives" (it's good news for shoppers)

House Un-American Activities Committee (Huac) anti-communist investigating body of the House of Representatives, often associated with "McCarthyism", although Joseph McCarthy was in fact head of the Senate permanent subcommittee on investigations

Housing Corporation

hovercraft

Hubble space telescope

Hudson Bay but **Hudson's Bay Company**

Human Genome Project

humanity, humankind not man, mankind *see gender issues*

hummus you eat it; **humus** you put it on the garden

humour, humorist, humorous

hundred years war

hunky dory

Huntington's disease formerly known as Huntington's chorea

huntsman a paid servant of the hunt, so do not use to mean hunters or hunt followers

hurricane lc, eg hurricane Katrina

Hutchison Telecommunications International (not Hutchinson) part of Hutchison Whampoa; **Hutchison Essar** in India, known as Hutch

hydroelectric

hyperbole don't overegg stories: strive instead for straight and accurate reporting; Guardian readers prefer the unvarnished truth *see sexing up*

hyperthermia hot; **hypothermia** cold

Aaaargh, no! PLEASE don't let the paper ape the awful US practice of missing out ampersands and adding commas, eg today's front page ("Young face tougher drink, smoking laws") – it's ugly and awful.

Chris Rogers, London

hyphens

Our style is to use one word wherever possible. Hyphens tend to clutter up text (particularly when the computer breaks already-hyphenated words at the end of lines).

This is a widespread trend in the language: "The transition from space to hyphen to close juxtaposition reflects the progressive institutionalisation of the compound," as Rodney Huddleston puts it in his Introduction to the Grammar of English.

Inventions, ideas and new concepts often begin life as two words, then become hyphenated, before finally becoming accepted as one word. Why wait? "Wire-less" and "down-stairs" were once hyphenated.

Words such as chatroom, frontbench, gameplan and housebuyer are all one word in the Guardian, as are thinktank (not a tank that thinks), longlist (not necessarily a long list) and shortlist (which need not be short).

Prefixes such as macro, mega, micro, mini, multi, over, super and under rarely need hyphens: examples are listed separately. Follow Collins when a word or phrase is not listed in this book.

There is no need to use hyphens with most compound adjectives, where the meaning is clear and unambiguous without: civil rights movement, financial services sector, work inspection powers, etc. Hyphens should, however, be used to form short compound adjectives, eg two-tonne vessel, stand-up comedian, three-year deal, 19th-century artist, etc. Also use hyphens where not using one would be ambiguous, eg to distinguish "black-cab drivers come under attack" from "black cab-drivers come under attack".

Do not use hyphens after adverbs ending in -ly, eg politically naive, wholly owned, but when an adverb is also an adjective (eg hard), the hyphen is required to avoid ambiguity – it's not a hard, pressed person, but a hard-pressed one; an ill-prepared report, rather than an ill, prepared one.

Use hyphens with short and common adverbs: much-needed grammar lesson, well-established principle of style (note though that in the construction "the principle of style is well established" there is no need to hyphenate)

"Iraq or Iran – what's our style?"
Freelance subeditor
(on a national paper –
not the Guardian)

ice age

ice-cream

iconic in danger of losing all meaning after more than 1,000 appearances in the Guardian in one year, employed to describe anything vaguely memorable or well-known – from Weetabix, Dr Martens boots and the Ferrero Rocher TV ads to Jimi Hendrix's final gigs, a plinth in Trafalgar Square and drains
see Icons, page 146

ID cards

ie no full points or comma, ie like this

if not can be ambiguous: does "it is the most beautiful castle in France, if not the whole of Europe" mean "and maybe in the whole of Europe" or "but not in the whole of Europe"?

IJ if a Dutch word starts with IJ then both letters are always capped (there is a waterway called the IJ so a lot of places have IJ in their name, eg IJsselmeer, IJmuiden, etc)

illegitimate do not use to refer to children born outside marriage (unless in a historical context, eg "the illegitimate son of Charles the Good")

iMac, iPod, iTunes

Imax cinemas

immaculate conception nothing to do with the birth of Jesus: it is the doctrine that Mary herself was conceived by her mother (St Anne) without the stain of original sin. The virgin birth is the doctrine of Christ's birth without a human father. This is one of our most frequent errors

immigrate to arrive in a country; **emigrate** to leave one

Immigration and Nationality Directorate may be called "the immigration service"

immune to not immune from

impact a noun, not a verb

Imperial College London (no commas) is no longer part of the University of London

impinge, impinging

impostor not imposter

impracticable impossible, it cannot be done; **impractical** possible in theory but not workable at the moment

impressionism, impressionist

in avoid such headline constructions as "Marconi chief in board clearout", which not only lacks a verb but is also ambiguous (is the chief clearing out the board or being cleared out with them?)

in or **on**? **in the team** not the US version "on the team"; **in Oxford Street** etc not "on Oxford Street"

inadmissible not -able

inchoate just beginning or undeveloped, not chaotic or disorderly

incidence amount, eg a high incidence of mistakes; **incident** event

incident be wary of this word: another — "attack" or "clash", for example — will often stand better in its place; within a couple of years of the massacre in Tiananmen Square the Chinese government was referring to it as an "incident" or even "alleged incident"

Icons

Bernard Manning's World Famous Embassy Club in Manchester

Nye Bevan

Yul Brynner

Brian Wilson

Capital FM

Alan Hawkshaw's Countdown theme

Debbie Does Dallas ("iconic tale of cheerleading and prostitution")

Viv Nicholson, 1960s football pools winner

the "trash-tastic" films of Russ Meyer and John Waters

grey wolves

red kites

footage of Bob Dylan flipping cards with the lyrics of Subterranean Homesick Blues on them

Adidas advertisements for the World Cup

Dutch formalism (in painting)

La Donna del Lago (opera by Rossini)

the words Rubber Soul on the Beatles album cover ("iconic piece of 60s calligraphy")

1976 biography of Christopher Columbus

logo of the 1948 Olympics

the fan magazine Photoplay

"Heineken's standard 3.4% brand"

test card recreated by Sky "to help guide viewers through their new high-definition service"

digital timer from the TV show 24

cut above the eye David Beckham sustained in 2003 after being hit by a flying boot kicked in anger by Alex Ferguson (an "iconic wound" – one of several for Beckham, we're told)

Keith Haring's image of the Radiant Child

giant limestone karsts encountered on a ferry from Phuket to Ko Phi Phi, Thailand

four jobs in 21st-century Britain, according to the Work Foundation: hairdressers, celebrities, management consultants and managers

video CV made by a Yale student and sent to a prospective Wall Street employer, subsequently posted on YouTube

rum punch

storm drains in Los Angeles

the design of Guardian Unlimited

income support

income tax

Independent Police Complaints Commission replaced the
Police Complaints Authority

index plural **indexes**, except for scientific and economic
indices

Indian placenames the former Bombay is now known as
Mumbai, Madras is now **Chennai**, Calcutta is now **Kolkata** and
Bangalore is now **Bengalooru**

indie music, films, etc; **Indy** short for the Independent, a
newspaper

indispensable not indispensible

Industrial Revolution

industrial tribunals have not existed since 1998, when they
became **employment tribunals**; they still appear in the pages of
the paper with embarrassing frequency despite regular
corrections from the readers' editor

infer/imply to infer is to deduce something from evidence; to
imply is to hint at something (and wait for someone to infer it)

infinite means without limit, not very large

infinitives *see split infinitives*

inflammable means the same as **flammable**, which we prefer;
the negative is **non-flammable**

initials no spaces or points, whether businesses or individuals,
eg WH Smith, PCR Tufnell

Inland Revenue *see Revenue & Customs*

inner city noun two words, adjective hyphenated: inner-city blues made Marvin Gaye wanna holler

innocent civilians the adjective is superfluous

innocuous

innuendo plural **innuendoes**

inoculate not innoculate

inpatient, outpatient

inquiry not enquiry

inshallah means "God willing" in Arabic

insignia are plural

insisted overused, especially in political stories; said should normally suffice

install, instalment

instil, instilled, instilling

Institute for Fiscal Studies

Institute for Public Policy Research

insure against risk; **assure** life; **ensure** make certain

insurgents, insurgency *see terrorism/terrorists*

International Atomic Energy Agency not "authority"; its director general is Mohamed ElBaradei; abbreviate to IAEA

international date line

interned imprisoned; **interred** buried (yes, we have got them confused)

internet net, web, world wide web *see Web style*

Interpol International Criminal Police Organisation (and a New York band)

InterRail

intifada

into or **in to**? one word if you go into a room, but two words in such sentences as I called in to complain, I listened in to their conversation and I went in to see my friend; **on to** two words *see on to*

in-tray, out-tray

introducing people

Never use the following construction to introduce a speaker or a subject: "Foreign secretary David Miliband said ... " Use the definite article and commas to separate the job from the name, like this: "David Miliband, the foreign secretary ... " (there is only one person with this specific post).

Commas are not used if the description is more general and could apply to more than one person, like this: "The health minister Dawn Primarolo said ... " (there are several health ministers); or like this: "The former paymaster general Dawn Primarolo said ... " (there have been many).

Another example: "Jonathan Glancey, the Guardian's architecture critic, gave his verdict ... " is correct; "The architecture critic Jonathan Glancey gave his verdict ... " is fine as well

Inuit not Eskimos; an individual is an **Inuk**

invalid means not valid or of no worth; do not use to refer to disabled or ill people

invariable, invariably unchanging; often used wrongly to mean hardly ever changing

iPod only when you are sure it is an Apple iPod; the generic term is **MP3 player** or **digital audio player**

Iraqi placenames

Use these spellings for Iraq's biggest cities and towns: Amara, Baiji, Baghdad, Baquba, Basra, Diwaniya, Dohuk, Falluja, Haditha, Hilla, Irbil, Kerbala, Kirkuk, Kut, Mosul, Najaf, Nassiriya, Ramadi, Rutba, Samarra, Samawa, Sulaimaniya, Tikrit (note that these transliterations do away with al- prefixes and the final H)

Ireland, Irish Republic not Eire or "Southern Ireland"

iridescent not irridescent

Irish Travellers capped, as they are recognised as a distinct ethnic group under race relations legislation

iron age, iron curtain

ironclad, ironfounder, ironmonger, ironworks

ironic, ironically

Do not use when what you mean is strange, coincidental, paradoxical or amusing (if you mean them say so, or leave it up to the reader to decide). There are times when ironic is right but too often it is misused, as in this typical example from the paper: "Santini's Tottenham won 2-0 at Nottingham Forest, ironic really with the north London club having a big interest in Forest's Republic of Ireland midfielder Andy Reid ... " (not that sport are the only, or biggest, offenders).

As Kingsley Amis put it: "The slightest and most banal coincidence or point of resemblance, or even just-perceptible absence of one, unworthy of a single grunt of interest, gets called 'ironical'."

The idiotic "post-ironic", which Amis would be glad he did not live to see, is banned

Isa individual savings account, but no need to spell it out

-ise not -ize at end of word, eg maximise, synthesise (exception: capsize)

Islam (means "submission to the will of God")
Muslims should never be referred to as "Mohammedans", as 19th-century writers did. It causes serious offence because they worship God, not the prophet Muhammad.

"Allah" is Arabic for "God". Both words refer to the same concept: there is no major difference between God in the Old Testament and Allah in Islam. Therefore it makes sense to talk about "God" in an Islamic context and to use "Allah" in quotations or for literary effect.

The holy book of Islam is the **Qur'an** (not Koran)

Islamist an advocate or supporter of Islamic fundamentalism; the likes of Osama bin Laden and his followers should be described as Islamist terrorists

Islamophobia

issue not a synonym for problem ("she has stylebook issues")

italics

Use roman for titles of books, films, etc; the only exception is the Review, which by special dispensation is allowed to ignore the generally sound advice of George Bernard Shaw:

"1 I was reading The Merchant of Venice.

2 I was reading 'The Merchant of Venice'.

3 I was reading *The Merchant of Venice*.

The man who cannot see that No 1 is the best-looking, as well as the sufficient and sensible form, should print or write nothing but advertisements for lost dogs or ironmongers' catalogues: literature is not for him to meddle with."

Use italics for foreign words and phrases (with roman translation in brackets); poetry *see poetry*; scientific names *see scientific names*

it's shortened form of it is or has: it's a big dog, it's been ages since I saw her

its possessive form of it: the dog is eating its bone

ITV1, ITV2, ITV3, ITV4

Ivory Coast not "the Ivory Coast" or Côte d'Ivoire; its nationals are **Ivorians**

Ivy League universities Brown, Columbia, Cornell, Dartmouth College, Harvard, Princeton, University of Pennsylvania, Yale

I suggest you reserve anything to do with icons to the Virgin Mary, Elvis Presley and a very limited number of people whose faces are recognised and revered, maybe also little figures on computer screens. Otherwise it becomes devalued and is just a trendy way of saying famous or memorable.

Bob Frankford,
Toronto

Jj

"What is the difference between
literature and journalism?
Journalism is unreadable and
literature is not read."

Oscar Wilde

Jj

J joules; **kJ** kilojoules

Jack Daniel's technically a Tennessee whiskey, not a bourbon

jack-in-the-box but **jack of all trades**

Jacuzzi TM, named after its US inventors, Roy and Candido Jacuzzi; call it a **whirlpool bath** unless you're sure it really is a Jacuzzi

jail not gaol

Jalalabad city in Afghanistan; **Jalal-Abad** is in Kyrgyzstan

JCDecaux no spaces

Jeep TM

Jehovah's Witness

jejune naive, unsophisticated (not necessarily anything to do with being young)

jellaba loose cloak with a hood, worn especially in north Africa and the Middle East

Jerez

jerry-builder

jetski

jewellery

jib triangular sail or arm of a crane; "I don't like the cut of his jib" means you don't like the look or manner of someone

jibe (not gibe) taunt

jihad used by Muslims to describe three kinds of struggle: an individual's internal struggle to live out the Muslim faith as well as possible; the struggle to build a good Muslim society; and the struggle to defend Islam, with force if necessary (holy war)

jobcentres are run by **Jobcentre Plus**

jobseeker's allowance

job titles are all lc, editor of the Guardian, governor of the Bank of England, prime minister, etc

jodhpurs

Joe Public, John Doe

john dory fish

John O'Groats

Johns Hopkins University not John Hopkins

Johnson Matthey plc metal specialist, not to be confused with **Johnson Matthey bank**

jokey not joky

Joneses as in "keeping up with the Joneses"; also note "the Joneses' house" (not the Jones' house)

Jonsson, Ulrika

judgment

judgment call use this phrase only if you delete the word "call"

July 7 2005 the London suicide bombings may be referred to as 7/7 in headlines; the bombers were Hasib Hussain, Mohammad Sidique Khan, Germaine Lindsay and Shehzad Tanweer

jumbo jet two words but **jump-jet**

junior abbreviate to **Jr** not Jun or Jnr, eg Sammy Davis Jr

just deserts not just desserts, unless you are saying you only want pudding

juvenile the Criminal Justice Act 1991 replaced this term with "youth", and raised the age at which you cease to be one from 17 to 18

I was a dedicated Independent reader until a few days ago when a friend lent me his copy of the Guardian stylebook. Oh dear, now I find myself reading that sentence several times over to make sure it doesn't contravene any of your rules or advices. How sad is that? And should that have been a question mark or an exclamation mark? Back to the Independent? No, apart from the useful advice, the sense of humour that runs through your book is far too much to my liking so at the very least I'll continue with my experiment with the Guardian in the hope that it is as readable as the book.

John Cannell, Brentwood, Essex

"The life of a journalist is poor, nasty, brutish and short. So is his style."

Stella Gibbons

Kk

Ka'bah cube-shaped shrine in the centre of the great mosque in Mecca towards which all Muslims face in prayer; the shrine is not worshipped but used as the focal point of the worship of God

Kabbalah

Kaiser Chiefs band from Leeds (no "the"); **Kaizer Chiefs** football club from Soweto; **Kaiser Wilhelm II** last German emperor and king of Prussia

Kajagoogoo 80s popsters best known for their No 1 hit Too Shy

kapok

Kara Suu (not Korasuv) town in Uzbekistan

Kashmir adjective **Kashmiri**; but **cashmere** fabric

Kasparov, Garry former world chess champion, born in Azerbaijan in 1963

Kathmandu capital of Nepal

Kazakhstan adjective **Kazakh**

kebabs a **doner** kebab is made using meat from a rotating spit; **shish** kebabs are made from skewered cubes of meat

Kefalonia not Cephalonia

Keir Hardie, James (1856-1915) first leader of the Labour party

Kellogg's Corn Flakes but **cornflakes** in general

key a useful headline word, but overused

keyring

key stage 1, 2, etc (education)

KFC not Kentucky Fried Chicken

K-For Nato peacekeeping force in Kosovo

Khachaturian, Aram (1903-78) Armenian composer

khaki

Khrushchev, Nikita (1894-1971) Soviet leader

kibbutz plural **kibbutzim**

kibosh

kick-off noun; **kick off** verb

kick-start noun or verb

Kilimanjaro not Mount Kilimanjaro

kilogram/s, kilojoule/s, kilometre/s, kilowatt/s abbreviate as **kg, kJ, km, kW**

King Edward potatoes

King's College, Cambridge comma

King's College London no comma

King's Cross

King's Lynn

Kings Road a road in Chelsea, west London; try not to call it "the Kings Road"; no apostrophe, although until 1830 it was a private royal road

Kingston upon Hull normally just **Hull**

Kingston upon Thames

Kirkcaldy not Kirkaldy; a town in **Fife**, not Fyfe

kir royale

kissogram

Kitemark TM on items approved by the British Standards Institution

KitKat

km/h kilometres an hour (not kph)

kneejerk reaction

Knightley, Keira actor

knockout noun; **knock out** verb

knots measure of nautical miles an hour, so do not say knots per hour

knowhow

knowledgable

koala not koala bear

Koh-i-noor diamond

koi not koi carp

Kolkata formerly Calcutta

Korean names like Hong Kong and Taiwanese names, Korean names are written in two parts with a hyphen, eg Kim Jong-il, Kim Dae-jung; on second mention they become Kim, etc (except in leading articles: Mr Kim, etc)

Kosovo, Kosovans adjective **Kosovan**, not Kosovar

kowtow

krona plural **kronor** Sweden; **krona** plural **kronur** Iceland; **krone** plural **kroner** Denmark; **krone** plural **kroner** Norway

krugerrands

Ku Klux Klan

kukri Gurkha knife

kung fu

KwaZulu-Natal

Kyrgyzstan adjective **Kyrgyz**

Kyrie Eleison

> The American basketball icon Michael Jordan is quoted as saying: "What Nike has done is turn me into a dream." As a card-carrying basketball fanatic from North Carolina, I can assure you he never said any such ungrammatical thing. It appears that the Guardian's style guide requires the conversion of American English ("Nike has … ") into Guardian English even when it is spoken by God (whom many of us honestly believe Michael Jordan to be).
>
> Jack Sandberg, Nags Head, NC

"Away with him! Away with
him! He speaks Latin."
**William Shakespeare,
Henry VI Part 2**

laager South African encampment; **lager** beer

La Coruña Spanish port

Lady Macbeth of Mtsensk Shostakovich opera, traditionally misspelt in the Guardian as Mtensk, with occasional variations such as Mtsenk

Lady Thatcher (and other ladies) not Baroness

lag pipes are lagged; other things lag behind

Lailat al-Miraj Islamic holy day

Lailat al-Qadr Islamic holy day, time for study and prayer

laissez-faire not italicised

Lake District or **the Lakes**

lambast

lamb's lettuce, lamb's wool

lamp-post

lance corporal

Land state of Federal German Republic; use state, eg Hesse, the German state

landmine

Land Registry government department that registers title to land in England and Wales

Land Rover

Land's End but the clothing firm is **Lands' End**

lang, kd Canadian singer

laptop

largesse

larva (plural **larvae**), insects; **lava**, volcanic magma; we often say the former when we mean the latter

La's, the defunct Liverpool rock band; keep apostrophe (abbreviation for Lads)

laser word dating from 1960 formed from the phrase "light amplification by stimulated emission of radiation", and an example of why not all acronyms need to be capped up

lasso noun (plural **lassos**) and verb: you lasso a horse with a lasso

last post

later often redundant, as context will inform the reader: "They will meet this month" rather than "They will meet later this month"

Latin

Some people object to, say, the use of "decimate" to mean destroy on the grounds that in ancient Rome it meant to kill every 10th man; some of them are also likely to complain about so-called split infinitives, a prejudice that goes back to 19th-century Latin teachers who argued that as you can't split infinitives in Latin (they are one word) you shouldn't separate "to" from the verb in English. Others might even get upset about our alleged misuse of grammatical "case" (including cases such as dative and genitive that no longer exist in English).

As the Guardian is written in English, rather than Latin, do not worry about any of this even slightly

latitude like this: 21 deg 14 min S

launderette but Stephen Frears' 1985 film was My Beautiful Laundrette

law lords may be female: we don't say "law ladies"

lawsuit

layby plural **laybys**

lay off does not mean to sack or make redundant, but to send workers home on part pay because of a temporary lack of demand for their product

lay waste a hurricane can lay waste an island, or lay an island waste, but it does not lay it to waste or lay waste to it (the word comes from the same root as devastate)

lbw (cricket)

Lea or **Lee**? the **river Lea** flows to the Thames; the **Lee Navigation canal** incorporates part of it; the **Lee Valley park** is the site for much of the 2012 Olympic development

leap year

Learjet

learned not learnt, unless you are writing old-fashioned poetry (he learned his tables, a message well learned)

led past tense of the verb "lead"; it is surprising how often such sentences as "he lead them to the scene of the crime" find their way into the paper

left, the, left wing, leftwinger nouns; **leftwing** adjective; **hard left, old left**

Legal Services Commission responsible for legal aid in England and Wales; in Scotland it is the **Scottish Legal Aid Board**

legal terms in England and Wales, in camera is now known as **in secret** and in chambers **in private**; a writ is a **claim form** and a plaintiff a **claimaint**; leave to appeal is **permission to appeal**.

Since the Children Act 1989, access has been known as **contact** and custody is known as **residence**; do not use the older terms

legionnaires' disease named after an outbreak at a conference of American Legionnaires

Leibovitz, Annie US photographer

lent past tense of lend; we sometimes say "leant" as in "a gritty drama, leant added authenticity by Jean Tournier's monochrome photography ... "

Leonardo da Vinci simply **Leonardo** on second mention

Le Pen, Jean-Marie Le Pen on second mention

lepers do not use: these days the term is regarded as inappropriate and stigmatising; prefer people with leprosy or, if they are being treated, leprosy patients

lese-majesty

less/fewer less means smaller in quantity, eg less money; fewer means smaller in number, eg fewer coins

letdown, let-up nouns; **let down, let up** verbs

leukaemia

level crossing

Levi's jeans; the company is **Levi Strauss**

Lévi-Strauss, Claude structural anthropologist

liaison

Lib Dems acceptable for Liberal Democrats after first mention and in headlines

libretto plural **librettos**

licence noun; **license** verb; you might enjoy your drinks in a **licensed premises** or take them home from an **off-licence**

Liechtenstein

lied German musical setting for a poem, plural **lieder**

Liège but adjective **Liégeois**

lieutenant colonel, lieutenant general abbreviate on second mention in leading articles to Col or Gen: Lieutenant Colonel Christopher Mackay, subsequently Col Mackay, etc

lifelong

lifesize not sized

lightbulb

lighthearted

light year a measure of distance, not time

likable not likeable

like/as if never use the former to mean the latter: "it looks as if he's finished" not "it looks like he's finished"

like/such as "like" excludes; "such as" includes: "Cities like Manchester are wonderful" suggests the writer has in mind, say, Sheffield or Birmingham; she actually means "cities such as Manchester".

Do not, however, automatically change "like" to "such as" – the following appeared in the paper: "He is not a celebrity, such as Jesse Ventura, the former wrestler ... "

likely he is likely to win or he will very likely win, not "he will likely win" – if you want to use that form, say "he will probably win"

lilliputian

limpid means clear or transparent, not limp

linchpin not lynchpin

lineup, lineout

liquefy not liquify

liquorice not licorice

listed buildings

In England and Wales, Grade I-listed (note cap G, roman numeral I) buildings are of exceptional interest; Grade II* are particularly important buildings of more than special interest; Grade II are of special interest, warranting every effort to preserve them. In Scotland and Northern Ireland these categories are replaced by the more logical Grade A, Grade B and Grade C

literally term used, particularly by sports commentators, to denote an event that is not literally true, as in "Manchester City literally came back from the dead" *see ironic, ironically*

Live 8 not Live8

Liverpool John Lennon airport

Lloyd's of London; **names** lc

Lloyds TSB bank

Lloyd-Webber, Lord but **Andrew Lloyd Webber**

loan noun; the verb is **lend**

loathe detest; **loth** unwilling, not loath

lobby take great care when using this term: unless you are writing about, say, the parliamentary lobby or US lobby system, it will at best sound vague and patronising, and at worst pejorative or offensive ("the Jewish lobby"). If you are talking about specific pressure groups, say who they are

local an adjective, not a noun: talk about local people rather than "locals"

loch Scottish; **lough** Irish

Lockerbie bombing in September 1988 killed 270 people; the two Libyans eventually put on trial for murder were Abdel Baset al-Megrahi and Al-Amin Khalifah Fhimah. Megrahi was convicted in 2001 and jailed for 27 years; his co-accused was acquitted

lock-in, lockout nouns; **lock in, lock out** verbs

logbook, logjam

London assembly elected body of 25 members whose role is to hold the mayor of London to account. Together, assembly and mayor constitute the **Greater London authority** (GLA); note there is no such organisation as the "Greater London assembly"

London boroughs and counties

Parts of the traditional counties of Essex, Middlesex, Kent and Surrey that are close to London retain the county link in their postal addresses (eg Bromley, Kent), even when they are administratively part of a London borough (eg the London borough of Bromley), and represented in the London assembly.

This leads to inconsistencies, as when we refer to "Chingford, Essex" in one story and "Chingford, east London" in another. It is hard to be totally consistent – the preferences even of people who live in such places may vary (according to how long they have lived there, for example).

In general, use London rather than the traditional counties – Ilford, east London; Bexley, south-east London, etc – unless a group or organisation specifically includes a county designation in its title

Londonderry use **Derry** and **Co Derry**

London Eye official name of the millennium wheel

London Paper, the not "thelondonpaper"

London's do not say "London's Covent Garden" (or London's anything else); it is **Covent Garden, London**

London School of Economics abbreviated to LSE after first mention

London Stock Exchange is also abbreviated to LSE, and there is no real way round this (especially for headlines); the context should make clear which we are talking about

London Transport Users Committee

Long Island iced tea

longitude like this: 149 deg 18 min E

longlist, shortlist

longtime adjective, as in longtime companion

look to used too often in place of hope to or expect to

looking-glass

lord chancellor the post was abolished in 2003, then reprieved; but the Lord Chancellor's Department was replaced by the Department for Constitutional Affairs, which in 2007 was absorbed into the new Ministry of Justice, at which point the lord chancellor also became secretary of state for justice

lord chief justice

lord lieutenant no hyphen, plural **lords lieutenant**

Lords, House of Lords but the house, not the House; **their lordships**

Lord's cricket ground

lottery, national lottery but **Lotto** and **National Lottery Commission**

lovable not loveable

Love's Labour's Lost

lowlife plural **lowlifes**, not lowlives (for an eloquent explanation, see Steven Pinker's Words and Rules)

loyalists (Northern Ireland)

Luiz Inácio Lula da Silva elected president of Brazil in 2002, he is normally known simply as **Lula**

lumpenproletariat

luvvies a silly cliche, best avoided

Luxembourgeois live in Luxembourg

luxury, luxurious

LVMH the luxury goods firm is, in full, **Moët Hennessy Louis Vuitton**

Lycra TM; the briefly fashionable term "lycra louts" led to complaints from the Lycra lawyers

lying in state no hyphens

Lynyrd Skynyrd late US rock band (named after a man called Leonard Skinner)

Lyon not Lyons

Like the Guardian, I am a Mancunian born and bred. I started buying the Manchester Guardian 60 years ago and have never stopped, even when I first came to Reading in 1958 and the paper was delivered a day late. Thank you for having made your guide available to a wider public. It will be a constant companion as I read my Guardian – you need an umpire to see that you stick to your own rules and it will be one of life's little pleasures to catch you out. (And there is a preposition to end a sentence and a conjunction to begin one.)

Peter Grantham, Reading

Mm

"I see my name spelt with one word, I want to slap and choke people. If you do that, you got to be a moron ... It's on every poster, every album and every ticket as two words. If you spell it as one, you're an idiot. Bottom line."

Meat Loaf

Mm

guardian style

Mac or **Mc**?

Andie MacDowell, Sue MacGregor, Kelvin MacKenzie, Shirley MacLaine, Murdo MacLeod

Sarah Macaulay (the prime minister's wife is now known as Sarah Brown), Sir Cameron Mackintosh, Elle Macpherson

Sir Paul McCartney, Sir Trevor McDonald, Ian McEwan, Ewan McGregor, Sir Ian McKellen, Malcolm McLaren, Coleen (not Colleen) McLoughlin

MacDonald, James Ramsay (1866-1937) first Labour prime minister, known as Ramsay MacDonald

mace, the (parliament); **Mace** riot control spray

machiavellian after Nicolo Machiavelli (1469-1527)

machine gun noun; **machine-gun** verb; **submachine gun**

Machu Picchu Peruvian "lost city of the Incas"

mackem refers both to a person from Sunderland, and their accent

Macmillan, Harold (1894-1986) Tory prime minister

MacMillan, Kenneth (1929-92) choreographer

MacNeice, Louis (1907-63) poet

Madame Tussauds no apostrophe, even though there was a Mme (Marie) Tussaud

madeira wine and cake

Madejski stadium home of Reading FC

Madison Square Garden (not Gardens) in New York City

Madras now known as **Chennai**

madrasa normally used to mean Islamic school, although in both Arabic and Urdu the word is used to refer to any kind of school

mafia

Mafikeng now spelt thus, though it was Mafeking when it was relieved in 1900

Magdalen College, Oxford

Magdalene College, Cambridge

magistrates court no apostrophe

maglev high-speed trains (it is short for magnetic levitation)

Magnum a .44 Magnum is a cartridge, not a gun (although Dirty Harry used a .44 Magnum revolver)

maharajah

Mahathir Mohamad prime minister of Malaysia from 1981 to 2003; Mahathir on second mention (except in leading articles, where he is Mr, not Dr, Mahathir)

mailbag, mailvan

mail train

mainland do not use to refer to Great Britain in reports about Northern Ireland

mainmast, mainsail

major a major case of overuse; avoid except in a military context: big, main and leading are among the alternatives

Mm

major general in leading articles, abbreviate on second mention to Gen: Major General Ben Summers, subsequently Gen Summers; otherwise just Summers

makeover, makeup no hyphens

Málaga

Malagasy inhabitant or inhabitants of **Madagascar** and the name of their language; the adjective for the country is **Madagascan**

Malaysian names generally the given name comes first, and Muslim Malays tend not to use surnames, so Mahathir Mohamad (Mahathir the son of Mohamad) becomes Mahathir on second reference. Chinese Malaysian names, like Singaporean names, are in three parts: eg Ling Liong Sik (Ling after first mention)

Mall, the in London

Mallorca not Majorca

Mamma Mia! musical show featuring Abba songs

mammon

mañana

manifesto plural **manifestos**

mankind use **humankind** or **humanity**

manoeuvre, manoeuvring

mantis plural **mantids**

Maori singular and plural

Mao Zedong Mao on second mention

marines, Royal Marines, but **US marines**

Marks & Spencer at first mention, then **M&S**

marquis not marquess, except where it is the correct formal title, eg Marquess of Blandford

Marrakech

Mars bar

Marseille not Marseilles

marshal (military rank) not marshall, a frequent error; a reader sent in this mnemonic: "Air Chief Marshal Marshall presided at the court martial of the martial arts instructor"

Marshall Aid

Martí, José (1853-95) writer and leader of Cuba's war of independence against Spain

martial law

Marxism, Marxist

Mary Celeste not Marie Celeste

Maryinsky theatre St Petersburg home of the Kirov Ballet

mass lc; mass is celebrated or said, not read

massacre the savage killing of large numbers of people, not Stockport County beating Macclesfield Town 5-0

massive massively overused

masterful imperious; **masterly** skilful

master's as in "I did my master's at UCL"

masthead

Mathews, Meg former model and ex-wife of Noel Gallagher; they have a daughter, Anais

matinee no accent

matins

matt matt finish, etc

maxidress

may or might?

The subtle distinctions between these (and between other so-called modal verbs) are gradually disappearing, but they still matter to many of our readers and can be useful.

may implies that the possibility remains open: "The Mies van der Rohe tower may have changed the face of British architecture forever" (it has been built); **might** suggests that the possibility remains open no longer: "The Mies tower might have changed the face of architecture for ever" (if only they had built it). Similarly, "they may have played tennis, or they may have gone boating" suggests I don't know what they did; "they might have played tennis if the weather had been dry" means they didn't, because it wasn't.

may also has the meaning of "having permission", so be careful: does "Megawatt Corp may bid for TransElectric Inc" mean that it is considering a bid, or that the competition authorities have allowed it to bid?

Mayday distress signal (from the French "*m'aidez!*"); **May Day** May 1

mayor of London or anywhere else, lc

MB megabytes (storage capacity)

Mbps megabits per second (communication speed); take care to get such terms right: we referred to a "2mbps internet connection" which, at two millibits a second, is about the speed of smoke signals

McAlpine note the "Sir" in the building and civil engineering company **Sir Robert McAlpine** (named after the baronet who founded it); not to be confused with **Alfred McAlpine** construction and support services

MCC, the not "MCC"

McCarthy & Stone retirement homes

McDonald's hamburgers; the possessive is the same word, eg "McDonald's new vegan-friendly image"

McJob defined by the OED as "an unstimulating, low-paid job with few prospects, esp one created by the expansion of the service sector"

McLuhan, Marshall (1911-80) Canadian author who coined the phrase "the medium is the message"

meanwhile usually means "here's a slight change of subject"

Meat and Livestock Commission

Meat Loaf sings; **meatloaf** doesn't

mecca as in "Ashton-under-Lyne is a mecca for tripe-eaters"

Mecca holy city in Saudi Arabia

Médecins sans Frontières international medical aid charity (don't describe it as French)

Medellín Colombia

media plural of **medium**: the media are sex-obsessed, etc; but a convention of spiritualists would be attended by **mediums**

Medicaid, Medicare are both US federal health insurance programmes, but Medicare primarily covers people over 65 and has no financial requirements for eligibility; Medicaid is targeted at those on low incomes

medieval not mediaeval

meet, met not meet with, met with someone

mega horrible; do not use

memento plural **mementoes**

memorandum plural **memorandums**

menage no accent

Menorca not Minorca

menswear, womenswear but the magazine is **Women's Wear Daily**

mental handicap, mentally handicapped, mentally retarded do not use: say person with learning difficulties

> On December 1 your paper ran an opinion "In praise of … metric measurements" and concluded: "Britain should stop muddling on with dual labelling and embrace metric." Yet today, five months later, your article on the security wall in Heiligendamm for the G8 conference gives dimensions of "length 7.5 miles, height 2.5 metres". Perhaps the unseasonally warm Centi-heit temperatures have affected your subediting.
>
> **Roz Denny, London**

mental health

Take care using language about mental health issues. In addition to such clearly offensive and unacceptable words as loony, maniac, nutter, psycho and schizo, expressions to avoid – because they stereotype and stigmatise – include victim of, suffering from, and afflicted by; "a person with" is clear, accurate and preferable to "a person suffering from". Never use schizophrenic to mean "in two minds", or as a noun. And avoid writing "the mentally ill" – say mentally ill people, mental health patients or people with mental health problems

merchant navy

Meridian ITV region; **Meridien** hotels

Messiaen, Olivier (1908-92) French composer

metaphor traditionally defined as the application to one thing of a name belonging to another, eg bowling blitz, economic meltdown, "every language is a temple in which the soul of those who speak it is enshrined" (Oliver Wendell Holmes)

method acting lc

Met Office

metres write metres out in full, to avoid confusion with million (an obvious exception would be in an article about athletics, eg she won the 400m)

metric system

The Guardian uses the metric system for weights and measures; exceptions are the mile and the pint. As understanding of the two systems is a matter of generations, conversions (in brackets) to imperial units should be provided wherever this seems useful, though usually one conversion – the first – will suffice. Imperial units in quoted matter should be retained, and converted to metric [in square brackets] if it doesn't ruin the flow of the quote.

It is not necessary to convert moderate distances between metres and yards, which are close enough for rough and ready purposes (though it is preferable to use metres), or small domestic quantities: two litres of wine, a kilogram of sugar, a couple of pounds of apples, a few inches of string. Small units should be converted when precision is required: 44mm (1.7in) of rain fell in two hours. But be sensible: don't convert a metric estimate into a precise imperial figure (round the conversion up or down). Tons and tonnes are close enough for most purposes to do without conversion; use tonnes (except in shipping tonnage).

Body weights and heights should always be converted in brackets: metres to feet and inches, kilograms to stones/pounds. Geographical heights and depths, of people, buildings, monuments, etc, should be converted, metres to feet. In square measurement, land is given in sq metres, hectares and sq km, with sq yards, acres or sq miles in brackets where there is space to provide a conversion. The floor areas of buildings are conventionally expressed in sq metres (or sq ft). Take great care in conversions of square and cubic measures: 2 metres is about 6.5 feet, but 2 sq metres is about 10.5 feet

Metropolitan police the Met at second mention; commissioner of the Metropolitan police, Met commissioner is acceptable; but note **Metropolitan Police Authority** (MPA)

mexican wave

meze not mezze (which is how it has appeared on the front page)

Miami Beach US city

mic abbreviation for microphone

mid-90s, mid-60s, etc

mid-Atlantic but **transatlantic**

midday

middle ages

middle America

Middle-earth (Tolkien) not Middle Earth

Middle East never Mid, even in headlines

middle England

Middlesbrough, Teesside not Middlesborough, Teeside

Midlands, east Midlands (but **East Midlands airport**), **West Midlands**

Midsummer Day June 24

midterm no hyphen

midweek

midwest (US)

MiG-21 Soviet Union-built fighter plane, still in use in some countries

might or **may**? *see may or might?*

Milad al-Nabi Islamic festival celebrating the birth of the prophet; many Muslims disapprove of celebrating this event

mileage

Militant tendency

militate or **mitigate**? to militate against something is to influence it (his record militated against his early release); to mitigate means to lessen an offence (in mitigation, her counsel argued that she came from a broken home)

millenary, millennium, millennia

Millennium Dome at first mention, then just **the dome**; reopened in 2007 as **the O2**

millennium wheel its official name is **London Eye**

million in copy use **m** for sums of money, units or inanimate objects: £10m, 45m tonnes of coal, 30m doses of vaccine; but **million** for people or animals: 1 million people, 23 million rabbits, etc; use **m** in headlines

mimic, mimicked, mimicking

min/mins contraction of minute/minutes

mineworker

minibus, minicab, miniskirt, minivan

MiniDisc TM

minimum plural **minima**

ministers

Minnelli, Liza note that it's "Liza with a Zee, not Lisa with an Ess"

minority ethnic (adjective) rather than ethnic minority

minuscule not miniscule

mis-hit, mis-sell but **misspell, misspent**

mistakable, unmistakable

misuse, misused

MLA member of the Northern Ireland assembly (it stands for member of the legislative assembly)

MLitt master of letters, not master of literature

Moby-Dick Herman Melville's classic is, believe it or not, hyphenated

Modern in the sense of Modern British, to distinguish it from "modern art"

Moët & Chandon

Mönchengladbach

moneys, moneyed

Mongol one of the peoples of Mongolia

mongooses (not mongeese) plural of mongoose

moniker

Monk, Thelonious (1917-82) American jazz pianist and composer, generally but erroneously referred to in the Guardian and elsewhere as "Thelonius"

Montenegro inhabited by **Montenegrins**

moon lc for the Earth's moon

Moors murders committed in the 1960s by Ian Brady and Myra Hindley

morbidity take care: can mean the state of being morbid (taking an unusual interest in death or unpleasant events); but morbidity, also known as the **morbidity rate**, also means the relative incidence of a disease in a specific locality

more than generally preferable to over: there were more than 20,000 people at the game, it will cost more than £100 to get it fixed; but she is over 18

More Than not MORE TH>N, which is how the insurance arm of Royal & Sun Alliance styles itself

Morissette, Alanis

morning-after pill

morris dancing

Morrisons for the stores, Wm Morrison Supermarkets is the name of the company; just to make it more confusing, **Morrison** is a support services company owned by AWG plc (Anglian Water)

morse code

mortgage borrower, lender the person borrowing the money is the mortgagor, the lender is both the mortgagee and the mortgage holder; to avoid confusion, call the mortgagor the mortgage borrower and the mortgagee the mortgage lender

mortise lock not mortice

mosquito plural **mosquitoes**

mother of parliaments the great 19th-century Liberal politician and Manchester Guardian reader John Bright described England, the country (not Westminster, the institution), as the mother of parliaments

mother of three etc, not mother-of-three; do not use unless relevant to the story

Mother's Day

Mötley Crüe, Motörhead include "heavy metal umlauts"

motorbike, motorcar, motorcycle

motor neurone disease

motorways just M1, etc, not M1 motorway

mottoes

movable

mph

MPs

Mr, Ms, Mrs, Miss

In leading articles: use the appropriate honorific after first mention (unless you are writing about an artist, author, journalist, musician, sportsman or woman, criminal or dead person, who take surname only); use Ms for women subsequently unless they have expressed a preference for Miss or Mrs.

Everywhere in the paper and website apart from leading articles: use first name and surname on first mention, and thereafter just surname *see honorifics*

MSP member of the Scottish parliament

Muhammad

Muslims consider Muhammad to be the last of God's prophets, who delivered God's final message. They recognise Moses and Jesus as prophets also.

The above transliteration is our style for the prophet's name and for most Muhammads living in Arab countries, though where someone's preferred spelling is known we respect it, eg Mohamed Al Fayed, Mohamed ElBaradei. The spelling Mohammed (or variants) is considered archaic by most British Muslims today

Muhammad Ali

mujahideen collective noun for people fighting a jihad; the singular is **mujahid**

mukhabarat secret police in the Arab world (it means "informers")

multicultural, multimedia, multimillion but **multi-ethnic**

mum or **Mum**? How is your mum? I don't know, I've not spoken to Mum for two years

Mumbai formerly Bombay, but no need to say so

Murphy's law "If there are two or more ways to do something, and one of those ways can result in a catastrophe, then someone will do it"; also known as sod's law

museums initial caps, eg British Museum, Natural History Museum, Victoria and Albert Museum (V&A on second reference), Metropolitan Museum of Art, etc

Muslim not Moslem

Muzak TM; better to call it easy listening, loungecore, or a similar variant

MW megawatts; **mW** milliwatts

myriad a large, unspecified number; use as an adjective (there are myriad people outside) or a noun (there is a myriad of people outside), but not "myriads of"

myxomatosis

The linguistic history of the "man" part of "mankind" does not limit it to male humans. "The proper study of humanity is people" does not have the same ring. I suppose your suggestion must be accepted, but it is sad that such a change has been forced by people determined to be insulted if possible. The problem is that, if a prejudice against the general sense of "man" is established, it can lead to misreadings. When Louis MacNeice wrote *Man is a spirit / Let the bells ring* he was not being sexist.
Michael Bulley, Chalon-sur-Saône, France

Military

For British brigades and divisions use cardinal numbers: 7 Armoured Brigade, 1 UK Armoured Division, 40 Commando, etc; for British battalions and regiments use ordinals, eg 2nd Battalion Royal Regiment of Fusiliers (for US divisions the style is as follows: 101st Air Assault, 82nd Airborne).

You go **aboard** a ship and when you are **on board** you may be welcomed aboard, but you sail or serve or travel **in** a ship. Note also that British ships are written "HMS Ark Royal", not "the HMS Ark Royal". When HMS is dropped, mariners shun the definite article, eg he served in Invincible, though inserting one can avoid ambiguities, eg he served in the Plymouth (the ship not the city).

A brief guide to weapons and equipment, etc:

ballistic missile has no wings or fins, and follows a ballistic trajectory, eg the Iraqi Scud

cruise missile missile with its own engine, best known is the Tomahawk

SAMs surface-to-air missiles

Harm high-speed anti-radiation missile, anti-SAM weapon

Jdam joint direct attack munition, the satellite-guided smartbomb

Moab massive ordnance air blast, nicknamed mother of all bombs

B-52, F-16 note hyphens

Tornado plural **Tornados**

Awacs airborne warning and control system, found on board the E-3 Sentry (a modified Boeing); Awacs is singular

Istar stands for intelligence, surveillance, target, acquisition and reconnaissance, a "real-time" intelligence-gathering system that aims to let decision makers respond to events as they occur

Lantirn stands for low altitude navigation and targeting infrared for night; the equipment allows fighters to fly at low altitudes, at night, and under the weather

Sead suppression of enemy air defences

A jargon-busting guide to the armed forces' command structure and organisation, ranks, and weapons and equipment follows:

Whitehall

The head of the armed forces is the **chief of the defence staff**, who is the chief military adviser to the defence secretary, equal in status to the permanent secretary of the Ministry of Defence on the civilian side. The rest of the defence staff comprises the vice-chief and the three service chiefs: chief of the naval staff, chief of the general staff, chief of the air staff, and their respective assistant chiefs. They and their various aides, advisers and experts (staff officers) make up the top-level HQ, at the MoD in Whitehall.

The MoD is divided into 11 sections headed by what it calls TLB (top level budget) holders, five of which are concerned with operations:

1 Chief of Joint Operations, responsible for all military operations, HQ at Northwood, north-west London
2 Navy: Commander in Chief Fleet
3 Army 1: Land Command
4 Army 2: General Officer Commanding, Northern Ireland
5 RAF: Strike Command

Each force has a personnel TLB, the other three are Central, Defence Procurement Agency and Defence Logistics Organisation.

Command structures in all three services are complicated by various joint commands and joint operations, either of two or more services or with other Nato/EU forces.

Royal Navy

The senior service: it was formed first, and its officers are senior to army and RAF officers of equivalent rank. The army, in turn, is senior to the RAF.

Command structure and organisation

Head: first sea lord and chief of the naval staff
Top body: the Admiralty Board, chaired by the defence secretary
Operational body: Navy Board, headed by first sea lord (1SL) and including commander in chief fleet, and second sea lord (deals with personnel, etc) and others

Work gets done by Battle Fleet Staff, headed by CinCFleet, who is a full admiral, with HQs in Portsmouth and Plymouth

Ships

Three aircraft carriers: they carry helicopters crewed by the Fleet Air Arm and Harrier jets crewed by a joint FAA and RAF command, and a Royal Marine commando unit. In a taskforce or other assembly of ships the carrier will have the admiral (or commodore) commanding on board, and will fly his flag, hence it is the flagship

Amphibious assault ships: land marines, etc, directly on land or by helicopter; like a small aircraft carrier

Destroyers and frigates: armed mainly with missiles and helicopters, for attack and defence against aircraft and other ships

Mine countermeasure vessels (MCMVs)

Assorted hydrographic survey ships, fisheries protection, patrol boats, etc

Submarine Service: ballistic missile subs (SSBN) are nuclear armed; fleet subs (SSN) are nuclear powered.

Training establishments on shore, including RN Reserve and University Royal Navy Units, are labelled HMS. The main bases (Portsmouth, Devonport, Clyde) are HMNB; Fleet Air Arm airfields are RNAS (royal naval air station) but also have a ship name, eg RNAS Yeovilton is also HMS Heron; NROs (naval regional offices/officers) are the regional flag wavers, each of four headed by a commodore.

Fleet Air Arm: organised in naval air squadrons, flying Merlin, Lynx and Sea King helicopters and Sea Harrier jump jets; its ranks are navy style.

Royal Fleet Auxiliary: tankers, supply, landing and repair ships; commanding officer is Commodore RFA, answering to CinCFleet, crews are civilian, ships are RFA (not HMS) Sir Galahad, etc.

Royal Marines are soldiers in ships (and planes), part of the navy but they have army-style ranks, eg colonel, major, sergeant. The main operational force is 3 Commando, which comprises three commando units, supported by Royal Engineers and Royal Artillery (army) commando units. Their main base and training centre is RM Poole. A branch of the Royal Marines is the **SBS** (Special Boat Service) whose fighters are special forces.

Ranks

Officers:

Admiral of the Fleet; Admiral (abbreviated to Adm on subsequent mentions); Vice Admiral (Adm); Rear Admiral (Adm). All four are flag officers, entitled to fly their flag in the ship (flagship) in which they are quartered. The captain of such a ship is a flag captain. A flag lieutenant is an admiral's aide-de-camp. Confusingly, the navy is liable to refer to/address any of these as flag for short

Commodore: likely to command, for example, a small force of ships or shore station (the title is also given to the chief captain of a shipping line)

Captain (abbreviated to Capt); Commander (Cmdr); Lieutenant Commander (Lt Cmdr); Lieutenant (Lt); Sub-Lieutenant (Sub Lt); Midshipman. The captain of a small ship will not have the rank of captain.

Ratings:

Warrant Officer (WO); Chief Petty Officer (CPO); Petty Officer (PO); leading and able ratings are usually addressed according to their trade or field of expertise, eg Leading Artificer (a naval term for engineer), Able Communications Technician, etc.

Weapons

Spearfish torpedo: wire and sonar-guided, homes on its target

Stringray torpedo: light, aircraft- or ship-borne

Paams: principal anti-air missile system, on destroyers, Aster 15 and Aster 30 (longer range) missiles

Sea Wolf (on frigates) and Sea Dart (destroyers): defensive anti-air missiles

Harpoon (frigate): anti-ship missile

Tomahawk (submarines): land attack cruise missile, 1,000-mile range

Goalkeeper: close range (up to 1,500 metres) defensive weapon system with seven-barrel Gatling gun firing at the rate of 70 rounds a second

Phalanx: last-chance 20mm Gatling gun, 3,000 rpm

114mm/4.5in Mk8 gun: the only real gun left in the navy, 21kg shell, 25 rpm, fitted to all frigates and destroyers

British army

Command structure and organisation

Head: chief of the general staff

Top body: the Army Board, chaired by the defence secretary

Main HQ is Joint Permanent Headquarters, Northwood (joint with the other services)

HQ Land Command, at Erskine barracks, Wilton, near Salisbury, commands fighting soldiers at home and abroad, and in addition there are:

HQ General Officer Commanding, Northern Ireland

plus HQ British Forces Cyprus, HQ British Forces Falkland Islands

The next level of command is the division. There are two operationally ready divisions, 1 (UK) Armoured Division, which is confusingly based in Germany, attached to Nato Allied Rapid Reaction Corps, and 3 (UK) Division, HQ Bulford, Wiltshire, part of the Nato Allied Rapid Reaction Corps. Numbers 2, 4 and 5 are administrative organisations, geographically based in Britain, capable of being bumped up if need be.

The next level is the brigade, historically consisting of three battalions/regiments of infantry or armour or artillery and support troops, but these days most units at most levels are mixed bunches. Of particular interest is 16 Air Assault Brigade, the newest and biggest (6,000) with a joint army/RAF HQ at Colchester; it is the primary rapid reaction force, including two Parachute Regiment battalions, one line infantry battalion, RAF and Army Air Corps units, artillery, engineers and other support services.

Corps are the professional organisations, both fighting and support. The infantry is technically a corps, though not often referred to as such, and there are the Royal Armoured Corps, Royal Corps of Logistics, etc.

Infantry

section: eight to 12 soldiers commanded by an NCO (corporal)

platoon: 25-40 soldiers commanded by a lieutenant, aided by a sergeant

company: three platoons and an HQ, 150 officers and men commanded by a major

battalion/regiment: three companies, a support company and an HQ company, 500-800 soldiers commanded by a lieutenant-colonel, assisted by an adjutant (usually a major). Some regiments have several battalions, ie 1, 2 and 3 Para. During the first and second world wars each regiment had many battalions. Many regiments have been disbanded: some amalgamated with others; some historical regimental names are preserved at company level (see Armoured Division)

The **SAS** is a regiment and counts as part of the infantry, but it is also designated special forces.

Armoured units

troop: four tanks, 12 troopers, commanded by a first or second lieutenant, a sergeant and two corporals, each of whom commands a tank

squadron: 14 tanks, commanded by a major (but there are reconnaissance squadrons with light armoured cars, etc)

regiment: 58 tanks, about 550 officers and troopers, commanded by a lieutenant colonel

brigade: three to four battalions/regiments grouped together with added support troops, commanded by a brigadier (in historical terms a brigade would be three infantry battalions but most of them are now made up of a wide range of fighting and support units of various sizes)

division: two to four brigades grouped together with added support troops, 16,000-30,000 soldiers commanded by a major general (30,000 may be theoretical, but the biggest is about 18,000, and others are as low as a couple of thousand). In addition, regiments are grouped in divisions, viz Guards Division, Scottish Division, Queen's Division, etc, and the Brigade of Gurkhas (which includes the Royal Irish regiment).

The Armoured Division includes the various remaining mounted units, Life Guards, Blues and Greys, assorted Hussars, Dragoons, Lancers, etc, retained for ceremonial purposes when the cavalry regiments were turned into tank regiments and gradually lost their individual identity.

Support troops are drawn from:
The Royal Regiment of Artillery (but it has many regiments, each with its own number, which are historical rather than an indication of the number currently in being). It is divided into batteries, not companies, privates are called gunners, corporals are bombardiers

Royal Engineers (a number of regiments, ie 21 Royal Engineers Regiment, plus battalions of the Royal Electrical and Mechanical Engineers (REME), which also tends to link with Logistics

The various corps, including:

Royal Corps of Logistics (transport and supply of ammunition, equipment, food, etc Formerly Transport Corps, formerly Royal Army Service Corps)

Royal Signals

Army Air Corps

Intelligence Corps

Royal Army Medical Corps (plus RA Dental and Veterinary Corps, and Queen Alexandra's Royal Army Nursing Corps)

Adjutant General's Corps (lawyers, administrators, teachers, Provost Branch, including Royal Military Police)

Ranks

Officers:

Field Marshal; General (abbreviated to Gen); Lieutenant General (Gen); Major General (Gen); Brigadier (Brig); Colonel (Col); Lieutenant Colonel (Col); Major (Maj); Captain (Capt); Lieutenant (Lt); Second Lieutenant (Lt).

Non-commissioned officers:

Warrant Officer First Class (WOI) – warrant officers hold their warrant, as commissioned officers hold their commission, from the sovereign; historically they were professional types rather than "gentlemen"; Warrant Officer Second Class (WOII), includes Regimental Quartermaster Sergeant (RQMS); Sergeant (Sgt) (Colour Sergeant, in cavalry/armoured regiments); Corporal (Cpl)/Bombardier (Bdr); Lance Corporal (L/Cpl) or Lance Bombardier (L/Bdr) in the artillery. Some NCOs have regimental/corps titles other than those indicated.

Note the Household Cavalry ranks of Corporal of Horse and Lance Corporal of Horse are abbreviated to CoH and LCoH, not Cpl and L/Cpl; a CoH corresponds to a sergeant in other regiments, so each time we use the wrong abbreviation we demote the soldier concerned.

According to the corps or regiment, the rank of Private (Pte) may be gunner, sapper (engineers), trooper (cavalry, armour), signalman, craftsman, driver, fusilier, ranger, kingsman, rifleman, airtrooper, etc.

Weapons and equipment

Light arms from the SA80 family – L85 individual weapon and L86 light support weapon – replace old-fashioned rifles and light machine guns; heavy machine gun; general purpose machine gun; light machine gun; Milan anti-tank weapon; 51mm and 81mm mortars; light anti-armour weapon (sits on the shoulder, looks like a bazooka); sniper rifles.

Armour: Challenger 2 main battletank; Warrior infantry fighting vehicle; Saxon armoured personnel carrier; Sabre armoured light recce vehicle; various others, eg Samaritan armoured ambulance, Samson armoured recovery vehicle (note that tanks, armoured personnel carriers and self-propelled guns look similar but have different roles. A tank's main role is to attack other tanks and armour. An armoured personnel carrier carries infantry, commanders, signallers or other support troops. Spata – stands for self-propelled artillery-tracked artillery – are big guns with their own engines).

Artillery: multiple launch rocket system; AS90 self-propelled gun (looks a bit like a tank, but tanks are primarily used on the move against other armour); L118 light gun; Starstreak high-velocity missile.

Aircraft: Apache attack; Bell 212; Gazelle and Lynx helicopters; Britten-Norman Islander plane.

Royal Air Force

Command structure and organisation
Head: chief of the air staff, senior to commander in chief strike command and deputy CinC strike command

Strike Command HQ at RAF High Wycombe, with three groups:
1 all strike aircraft
2 all support aircraft
3 Joint Force Harrier, mix of RAF and navy, commanded by a naval officer;
UK Combined Air Operations Centre at High Wycombe works with RAF, RN and Nato forces to scamble the jets if the missiles start coming in

The basic units are squadrons, those at the sharp end being strike/attack and offensive support; air defence and airborne early warning, and reconnaissance. HQs, airfields and other establishments are RAF stations, eg RAF Boulmer.

Ranks

Officers: Marshal of the Royal Air Force; Air Chief Marshal; Air Marshal; Air Vice-Marshal; Air Commodore (equivalent to navy commodore and army brigadier); Group Captain (Group Capt, equivalent to captain, colonel); Wing Commander (Wing Cdr, = commander, lieutenant colonel); Squadron Leader (Sqn Ldr, = lieutenant commander, major); Flight Lieutenant (Flt Lt, = lieutenant, captain; Flying Officer, (= sub-lieutenant, lieutenant); Pilot Officer (Plt Off, = midshipman, second lieutenant – except that midshipmen are junior to their army and air force counterparts).

Other ranks:
Master Aircrew (= warrant officer, WOI); Warrant Officer (WO, = warrant officer, WOI); Flight Sergeant (FS, = chief petty officer, staff corporal, staff sergeant); Chief Technician (Ch Tech, = chief petty officer, staff corporal, staff sergeant); Sergeant (Sgt, = petty officer, sergeant, corporal of horse); Corporal (Cpl, = leading rate, corporal, bombardier); Junior Technician (Jr Tech, = able or ordinary rate, private or its equivalents, as are the remaining ranks); Senior Aircraftman/Aircraftwoman and Leading Aircraftman/Aircraftwoman.

Equipment

Offensive aircraft:
Harrier single-seat attack, vertical take off and landing, general purpose bomb, cluster bombs, laser-guided bombs, anti-tank bombs
Jaguar single-seat attack and recce, general purpose bomb, cluster bombs, guided bomb, rockets, cannon, defensive air-to-air missiles
Tornado GR4 twin seat, swing wing, supersonic, guided bombs, cruise missiles
Typhoon (Eurofighter) upcoming replacement for Jaguar and Tornado F3, bristling with all the above weapons

Defensive aircraft:
Sentry ex-Boeing 707, flying radar station
Tornado F3 twoseater supersonic, air-to-air and anti-radar missiles

Recce/marine patrol:
Canberra 1940s bomber, now high-altitude recce
Nimrod based on Comet, the first jetliner

Transport:
Globemaster, Hercules, Tristar, VC10

Weapons
air-to-air missiles: Asraam, Aim-9 Sidewinder, Amraam, Skyflash
anti-shipping: Harpoon, Stingray
short-range air-to-surface (gp bombs): CVR-7 1,000lb bomb, Paveway II and III,
Enhanced Paveway (guided gp bombs), Maverick (missile)
long-range air-launched missiles: Alarm, Brimstone, Storm Shadow
surface-to-air (defensive) missile system: Rapier
cannon: Aden 30mm/1,200-1,400 rounds a minute (the rate of fire, the ammo
box carries only 150 rounds); Mauser 27mm, 1,000/1,700 rounds a minute
rate of fire.

Finally, here is our style for US aircraft that played a big part in the wars in Iraq
and Afghanistan: F-14 Tomcat, F-15 Eagle, F-16 Fighting Falcon, F/A-18
Hornet/Super Hornet, F-117 Nighthawk stealth fighter, B-52 Stratofortress, B-2
stealth bomber, B-1B Lancer

"Trust your editor, and you'll
sleep on straw."

John Cheever

Nabokov, Vladimir (1899-1977) Russian-born author of Lolita;
not Nabakov

nailbomb

naive, naively, naivety

names

Prominent figures can just be named in stories, with their function at
second mention: "Alistair Darling said last night ... " (first mention);
"the chancellor added ... " (subsequent mentions).

Where it is thought necessary to explain who someone is, write
"Bryan Robson, the Sheffield United manager, said" or "the Sheffield
United manager, Bryan Robson, said".

In such cases the commas around the name indicate that there is
only one person in the position, so write "the Tory leader, David
Cameron, said" (only one person in the job), but "the former Tory
leader Michael Howard said" (there have been many).

Do not leave out the definite article in such constructions as "style
guru David Marsh said ... " It should be "The style guru David
Marsh" (if there are other style gurus) or "David Marsh, the style
guru ... " (if you feel only one person merits such a description)

Nasa National Aeronautics and Space Administration, but no
need to spell out

nation

Do not use when you mean country or state; reserve nation to
describe people united by language, culture and history so as to form
a distinct group within a larger territory. And beware of attributing
the actions of a government or a military force to a national
population (eg, "The Israelis have killed 400 children during the
intifada"). Official actions always have opponents within a
population; if we don't acknowledge this, we oversimplify the
situation and shortchange the opponents

Nn

national anthem
– National
Offender
Management
Service

guardian style

national anthem

National Archives the former Public Record Office, now merged with the Historical Manuscripts Commission

National Association of Schoolmasters Union of Women Teachers (NASUWT) call it "the union" after first mention if you want to avoid using these unlovely initials; note that an "and" seems to be missing somewhere

National Audit Office

national curriculum

National Endowment for Science, Technology and the Arts Nesta after first mention

National Grid transmits electricity and gas

National Health Service but **NHS** or **health service** are normally sufficient

National Hunt horseracing

National Institute for Health and Clinical Excellence Nice after first mention

national insurance

nationalists (Northern Ireland)

national lottery

National Offender Management Service formed in 2004 from a merger between the prison and probation services, it moved from the Home Office to the Ministry of Justice in 2007; Noms after first mention (but note that in the US, Noms stands for national outcomes measurement system)

national parks lc, eg Peak District national park, Yellowstone national park

National Savings & Investments may be abbreviated to NS&I

national service peacetime conscription in the UK lasted from 1949 until 1960

Native Americans Geronimo was a Native American (not an American Indian or Red Indian); George Bush is a native American

Nato North Atlantic Treaty Organisation, but no need to spell out

naught nothing; **nought** the figure 0

Navarro-Valls, Joaquín former Vatican spokesman

navy but **Royal Navy**

Nazi but **nazism**

Neanderthal man scientific name and style is *Homo neanderthalensis*

nearby one word, whether adjective or adverb: the pub nearby; the nearby pub

nearsighted, nearsightedness

neocon, neoconservative, neoliberal

neophilia

Even if you have always wanted to appear in Private Eye, resist the temptation to write such nonsense as "grey is the new black", "billiards is the new snooker", "Barnsley is the new Tuscany", etc

nerve-racking

Nestlé

Netherlands, the not Holland, which is only part of the country; use Dutch as the adjective. Exception: the Dutch football team is generally known as Holland

nevertheless

new often redundant, as in "a new report said yesterday"

new age travellers

Newcastle-under-Lyme hyphens; **Newcastle upon Tyne** no hyphens

New Deal capped up, whether you are talking about Franklin D Roosevelt's job creation policies in the 1930s or Gordon Brown's more recent version

newfound

New Labour but **old Labour**

news agency

newsagent, newsprint, newsreel

newspaper titles the Guardian, the New York Times, etc; do not write "the Sun newspaper", etc: patronising and unnecessary

New Testament

new year lc, but **New Year's Day, New Year's Eve**

New Year honours list

New York City but **New York state**

next of kin

NHS National Health Service, but not necessary to spell out; health service is also OK

Nichpa National Infection Control and Health Protection Agency

Nietzsche, Friedrich Wilhelm (1844-1900) German philosopher; occasionally misspelt, even in the Guardian

Nigerian names surnames do not exist in the north of Nigeria: a typical name would be Isa Sani Sokoto (Isa the son of Sani who comes from the town of Sokoto); so best to write in full

nightcap, nightdress, nightfall, nightgown, nightshade, nightshirt but **night-time**

nimby, nimbyism it stands for "not in my backyard"

Niño, El

niqab veil that covers the face apart from the eyes

Nissan cars; **Nissen** hut

No 1 in the charts, the world tennis No 1, etc

No 10 (Downing Street)

no plural **noes**

Nobel prize Nobel peace prize, Nobel prize for literature, etc

no-brainer means something along the lines of "this is so obvious, you don't need a brain to know it" not "only someone with no brain would think this"

no campaign, yes campaign not No campaign, "no" campaign or any of the other variants

no doubt that, no question that are opposites: "There was no doubt that he was lying" means he was lying; "There was no question that he was lying" means he wasn't, although the two are routinely confused

Noel no accent on Noel as in Christmas (The First Noel, not "Nowell"); use an accent if that's how the person spells his or her name: Noël Coward had one, Noele Gordon didn't

no-fly zone

no man's land no hyphens

noncommissioned officer

nonconformist

none

It is a (very persistent) myth that "none" has to take a singular verb: plural is acceptable and often sounds more natural, eg "none of the current squad are good enough to play in the Premiership", "none of the issues have been resolved"

nonetheless

no one not no-one

Nordic countries Denmark, Norway, Sweden, Finland and Iceland

north north London, north Wales, north-west England, the north west, etc

Nn

north-east England Tyneside (Newcastle), Wearside (Sunderland), Teesside (Middlesbrough); we often confuse these or get them wrong in some way that makes it look as if the farthest north-east we have ventured is Stoke Newington

northern hemisphere

northern lights also known as aurora borealis; the southern hemisphere counterpart is aurora australis

north of the border avoid this expression: the Guardian is a national newspaper

north pole

North-West Frontier province Pakistan

North York Moors national park; but **North Yorkshire Moors railway**

nosy not nosey

notebook, notepaper

noticeboard

Nottingham Forest, **Notts County**

Notting Hill carnival

now useful for emphasis, but is now used far too often

npower retail arm of RWE npower; nothing to do with nuclear power

numbers

Spell out from one to nine; numerals from 10 to 999,999; thereafter
use m or bn for sums of money, quantities or inanimate objects in
copy, eg £10m, 5bn tonnes of coal, 30m doses of vaccine; but million
or billion for people or animals, eg 1 million people, 3 billion rabbits,
etc; spell trillion in full at first mention, then tn; in headlines use m,
bn or tn

numeracy

Numbers have always contained power, and many a journalist will
tremble at the very sight of them. But most often the only maths we
need to make sense of them is simple arithmetic. Far more important
are our critical faculties, all too often switched off at the first sniff of a
figure.

It's easy to be hoodwinked by big numbers in particular. But are
they really so big? Compared with what? And what is being assumed?
A government announcement of an extra £X million a year will look
far less impressive if divided by 60 million (the British population)
and/or 52 (weeks in the year). That's quite apart from the fact that it
was probably trumpeted last week already, as part of another, bigger
number. We have to be aggressive when interpreting the spin thrown
at us.

The legal profession has, in the same way, been forced to put DNA
evidence in the dock. If the probability of the accused and the culprit
sharing the same genetic profile is one in 3 million, then there are 19
other people in Britain alone who share the same DNA "match".

Never invent a big figure when a small one will do. Totting jail
sentences together ("the six men were jailed for a total of 87 years") is
meaningless as well as irritating. Similarly, saying that something has
an area the size of 150 football pitches, or is "eight times the size of
Wales", is cliched and may not be helpful.

Here is an easy three-point guide to sidestepping common
"mythematics" traps:

1 Be careful in conversions, don't muddle metric and imperial, or linear, square and cubic measures. Square miles and miles square are constantly confused: an area 10 miles square is 10 miles by 10 miles, which equals 100 square miles.

2 Be extremely wary of (or don't bother) converting changes in temperature; you run the risk of confusing absolute and relative temperatures, eg while a temperature of 2C is about the same as 36F, a temperature change of 2C corresponds to a change of about 4F.

3 When calculating percentages, beware the "rose by/fell by X%" construction: an increase from 3% to 5% is a 2 percentage point increase or a 2-point increase, not a 2% increase

Nuremberg

I've just bought the Guardian stylebook and think it's great. I took it to read on the train and I had to stop myself from saying out loud: "Yes, that's right – I agree." You've confirmed things I already know, plus I learned lots of things I didn't know that I didn't know. I particularly liked your equalities, age, and gender terminology advice – absolutely spot-on.

Julia Buckland, Derby

"I try to leave out the parts that
people skip."

Elmore Leonard

O2, the (cap O, not the number 0) is the new name for the former Millennium Dome

OAPs, old age pensioners do not use: they are **pensioners** or **old people**; note also that we should take care using the word elderly — it should not be used to describe anyone younger than 70

obbligato not obligato

O'Brian, Patrick author of Master and Commander

obscenities *see swearwords*

obtuse "mentally slow or emotionally insensitive" (Collins); often confused with **abstruse** (hard to understand) or **obscure**

Occam's razor philosophical principle, attributed to the 14th-century English friar William of Ockham, that broadly means prefer the simplest explanation, adopting the one that makes the fewest assumptions and "shaving away" the rest

occupied territories

occurred two Rs

Oceania a preferable term to Australasia, it is sometimes divided into Near Oceania and Remote Oceania, and comprises, according to the UN:
Australia/New Zealand
Melanesia (Fiji, New Caledonia, Papua New Guinea, Solomon Islands, Vanuatu)
Micronesia (Guam, Kiribati, Marshall Islands, Federated States of Micronesia, Nauru, Northern Mariana Islands, Palau)
Polynesia (American Samoa, Cook Islands, French Polynesia, Niue, Pitcairn, Samoa, Tokelau, Tonga, Tuvalu, Wallis and Futuna Islands)

oceans, seas capped up, eg Atlantic Ocean, Red Sea

OECD Organisation for Economic Cooperation and Development, but not normally necessary to spell out

oedipal complex; the female equivalent is the **electra complex**

Ofcom Office of Communications; call it the broadcasting and telecommunications regulator or something similar

Offa Office for Fair Access (to higher education)

Offa eighth-century king of Mercia, best known for Offa's Dyke, a giant earthwork that separated the kingdom from Powys

offbeat, offhand, offside

Office for National Statistics ONS on second mention

Office of Fair Trading OFT on second mention

Office of the Deputy Prime Minister replaced in 2006 by the Department for Communities and Local Government, which dropped the "Department for" a year later *see departments of state*

off-licence

Ofgem regulates the gas and electricity markets in Britain

Ofsted Office for Standards in Education, but normally no need to spell out

Ofwat regulates the water and sewerage industry in England and Wales

Oh! not O!

oilfield

oil painting

I've seen some choice grocer's apostrophes in the past, but I think "The Orkney's" in today's Guardian takes the biscuit.

Tom Maxwell,
London

oil production platform for production of oil; **oil rig** for exploration and drilling

oilseed rape

OK is OK; okay is not

old Labour but **New Labour**

Old Testament

O-levels GCE O-levels and CSEs were combined in 1986 to become GCSEs

Olympic games or just **Olympics** or **the games**

omelette

one in six, one in 10 etc should be treated as plural. There are good grammatical and logical reasons for this. Compare "more than one in six Japanese is 65 or older … " with "more than one in six Japanese are 65 or older … "

Grammatically, we are talking not about the noun "one" but the noun phrase "one in six", signifying a group of people. Logically, the phrase represents a proportion – just like "17%" or "one-sixth", both of which take plural verbs. "Two out of every seven" and "three out of 10" take plurals too, functioning identically.

"One in six is … " is also unnecessarily (and possibly misleadingly) specific, implying that of any six people from the group you take, exactly one will be as described. "One in six" means one-sixth on average over the whole group, and a plural verb better reflects this. We wouldn't say "Only 1% of Republican voters is able to point to Iraq on a map" just because there's a "one" in there

one nation Tory

Onetel UK telecom company, not One.Tel, which is Australian

ongoing prefer continuous or continual

online

only can be ambiguous if not placed next to the word or phrase modified: "I have only one ambition" is clearer than "I only have one ambition"; however, be sensible: do not move the "only" in I Only Have Eyes for You when discussing the greatest songs of all time (the Flamingos' version was ranked 157th by Rolling Stone magazine)

on to not onto; Kingsley Amis, perhaps slightly overstating the case for this, argued: "I have found by experience that no one persistently using onto writes anything much worth reading" *see into*

Op 58, No 2 music style

Opec Organisation of the Petroleum Exporting Countries, but not necessary to spell out

opencast

ophthalmic

opossum

opposition, the

or

Do not use "or" when explaining or amplifying – rather than "the NUT, or National Union of Teachers" say "The NUT (National Union of Teachers)" or, even better, "The National Union of Teachers" at first mention and then just "the NUT" or "the union"

Oo

ordinance direction, decree

Ordnance Survey Britain's national mapping agency ("ordnance" because such work was originally undertaken by the army)

Orkney not "the Orkney Isles" or "the Orkneys"

Ottakar's bookshop taken over by Waterstone's

Ötzi the Iceman Europe's oldest natural human mummy (dated to about 3300BC), found in the Alps in 1991

Ouija TM the generic name most commonly used, though not very satisfactory, is "talking board"

outback (Australia)

outed, outing take care with these terms: if we say, for example, that a paedophile was outed, we are equating him with a gay person being outed; use exposed or revealed instead

outgrow, outgun, outmanoeuvre

outpatient, inpatient

St Thomas' hospital in south London boasts the following styles, all on signs within a few yards of each other: Out Patients, Out-Patients, Outpatients, and outpatients

outre no accent

outside not "outside of"

outward bound use a safer term such as outdoor adventure or adventure training: we have been sued twice for reporting that people have died on "outward bound" courses that were nothing to do with the Outward Bound Trust

over not overly

overestimate, overstate take care that you don't mean underestimate or understate (we often get this wrong)

overreact, override, overrule and most other words with the prefix "over" do not need a hyphen

overweening not over-weaning, overweaning

Oxford comma a comma before the final "and" in lists: straightforward ones (he had ham, eggs and chips) do not need one, but sometimes it can help the reader (he had cereal, kippers, bacon, eggs, toast and marmalade, and tea), and sometimes it is essential: compare

I dedicate this book to my parents, Martin Amis, and JK Rowling

with

I dedicate this book to my parents, Martin Amis and JK Rowling

oxymoron does not just vaguely mean self-contradictory; an oxymoron is a figure of speech in which apparently contradictory terms are used in conjunction, such as bittersweet, "darkness visible" (Paradise Lost), "the living dead" (The Waste Land); one of Margaret Atwood's characters thought "interesting Canadian" was an oxymoron

My husband just woke me up to complain: "There is a solecism in a Guardian headline!" ("Brown invites outsiders onto Labour team", front page.) A bitter fight ensued and he has me doubting myself now – is it, or is it not, ever acceptable to use "onto" as a single word?
Teresa Hewitt, Toddington, Gloucestershire

"Journalism is the ability to meet
the challenge of filling space."
Rebecca West

pace Latin tag meaning "by the leave of", as a courteous nod to the views of a dissenting author, or "even acknowledging the existence of", not "such as"

Pacific Ocean

PacifiCorp part of ScottishPower

paean song of praise; **paeon** metrical foot of one long and three short syllables; **peon** peasant

page 1, etc, but **Page 3 girl**

País, El

palate roof of the mouth, sense of taste; **palette** used by an artist to mix paint; **pallet** hard bed, wooden frame moved by forklift truck

Palestine best used for the occupied territories (the West Bank and Gaza); if referring to the whole area, including Israel, use "historic Palestine" (but Palestine for historical references to the area prior to 1948)

Palestinian Authority the authority on second reference

palindrome A man, a plan, a canal. Panama!

Palme d'Or (Cannes film festival)

Palme, Olof (1927-86) Swedish prime minister who was assassinated in a Stockholm street (not Olaf)

Palmer-Tomkinson, Tara

P&O

panama hat

Pandora's box

panel, panelled, panelling

panjandrum a pretentious or self-important person in authority

Panjshir valley of Afghanistan

pantyhose not pantihose

paparazzo plural **paparazzi**; named after a character in Fellini's 1960 film La Dolce Vita

paperboy, papergirl but **paper round**

papier-mache

parallel, paralleled, 49th parallel, etc

Paralympic games or **Paralympics**

parentheses *see brackets*

Parker Bowles, Camilla no hyphen

Parkinson's disease

Parkinson's law "Work expands so as to fill the time available for its completion"

parliament, parliamentary but cap up those parliaments referred to by their name in the relevant language, eg Knesset, Folketing, Duma, etc

Parma ham but **parmesan** cheese

Parthenon marbles official name, recognised by both Britain and Greece, for the Elgin marbles

part-time

partwork one in a series of regularly published supplements or magazines

party lc in name of organisation, eg Labour party

Pashtuns (singular **Pashtun**; they speak **Pashtu)** make up about 40% of the Afghan population (called Pathans during the British Raj); a significant proportion of Pakistan's population is also Pashtun

passerby plural **passersby**

passive voice strive for active verbs, especially in headlines: compare "the mat was sat upon by the cat" with "the cat sat on the mat"

Passport Agency now part of the Identity and Passport Service

password

pasteurise

pâté with accents

Patent Office now the **Intellectual Property Office**, responsible for copyright, designs, patents and trademarks

patients are discharged from hospital, not released

payback, payday, payoff, payout

peacekeeper, peacetime

Peak District

Pearl Harbor use American English spellings for US placenames

peccadillo plural **peccadilloes**

pedaller cyclist; **peddler** drug dealer; **pedlar** hawker

pedalo plural **pedalos**

Pedro Ximénez white grape grown in Spain (and type of sherry); **Pedro Giménez** white grape grown in South America

peers

Avoid writing "Lord Asquith's Liberal government", or "Lady Thatcher took power in 1979"; when talking about people before they were given peerages use their names/titles at the time (eg Herbert Asquith, Mrs Thatcher).

Also avoid the construction "Lady Helena Kennedy": in this case we would write Lady Kennedy or Helena Kennedy, or – if really pushed – Lady (Helena) Kennedy (but never Baroness Kennedy)

peewit

peking duck

pendant noun; **pendent** adjective

peninsula noun; **peninsular** adjective

penknife

pensioners do not call them "old age pensioners" or "OAPs"; **older people** is preferable to "elderly people" or (even worse) "the elderly"

peony flower

Pepsi-Cola TM; a brand of **cola**; the company is **PepsiCo**

Pp

per avoid; use English: "She earns £30,000 a year" is better than "per year". If you must use it, the Latin preposition is followed by another Latin word, eg per capita, not per head. An exception is miles per hour, which we write mph

per cent % in headlines and copy

percentage rises

Probably our most common lapse into "mythematics": an increase from 3% to 5% is a 2 percentage point increase or a 2-point increase, not a 2% increase; any sentence saying "such and such rose or fell by X%" should be considered and checked carefully

Pérez de Cuéllar, Javier Peruvian diplomat and former UN secretary general

performance-related pay

Performing Right Society not Rights

permissible

Peronists supporters of the nationalist/populist ideology of the late Argentinian president Juan Domingo Perón

personal equity plan Pep

persons No! They are people (can you imagine Barbra Streisand singing "Persons who need persons"?)

Perspex TM

peshmerga Kurdish armed fighters (it means "those who face death")

phenomenon plural **phenomena**

Philippines inhabited by **Filipinos** (male) and **Filipinas** (female); adjective **Filipino** for both sexes, but **Philippine** for, say, a Philippine island or the Philippine president

Philips electronics; **Phillips** auctioneers, screwdriver; **Phillips & Drew** since 2002, part of UBS Global Asset Management

philistine

Phnom Penh

phone no apostrophe

phoney

phosphorous adjective; **phosphorus** noun

photocall, photocopy, photojournalist

photo-finish

photo opportunity

pi the ratio of the circumference of a circle to its diameter, as every schoolgirl knows

picket noun (one who pickets), not picketer; **picketed, picketing**

piecework

pigeonhole verb or noun

pigsty plural **pigsties**

Pilates

pill, the (contraceptive)

pillbox

Pimm's the most popular version is Pimm's No 1 cup, which has gin as its base (the others are or were No 2, whisky; No 3, brandy; No 4, rum; No 5, rye; and No 6, vodka)

pin or **pin number** not Pin or PIN number

pinstripe suit, etc, not pinstriped

pipebomb

pipeline

Pissarro, Camille (1830-1903) French impressionist painter; his son Lucien (1863-1944) was also an artist

pixelated an image divided into pixels, the basic unit of representation on a television or computer screen, or to display a person or object in pixels to disguise their identity

pixilated drunk

placename

plane a higher plane, not a higher plain (unless literally)

planets cap up planets of our solar system: Mercury, Venus, Earth, Mars, Jupiter, Saturn, Uranus and Neptune; note that Pluto is now classified as a dwarf planet, along with Ceres and Eris; the sun and the Earth's moon are lc, but named moons are capped up: Europa, Io, etc

planning not "forward planning"

Planning Inspectorate handles planning inquiries and appeals in England and Wales

plaster of paris

plateau plural **plateaux**

plateglass

playbill, playgoer, playwright

Play-Doh TM but you can say play-dough

playing the race card an overused phrase

play-off

PlayStation

plc not PLC

plea, pledge words used all the time by journalists (particularly when writing headlines), but only rarely by normal people

pleaded not pled

plebeian not plebian, one of our most common errors

pocketbook, pocketknife but **pocket money**

poet laureate

poetry

Separate the lines with spaces and a slash; italics are acceptable: *I struck the board and cry'd, 'No more; | I will abroad.' | What, shall I ever sigh and pine? | My lines and life are free; free as the rode, | Loose as the winde, as large as store.*

You write that "Lord Black and his colleagues shrunk the company" while "his long-serving business partner has pled guilty to fraud." Since the film Honey, I Shrunk the Kids it seems that the Guardian has forgotten the word "shrank", which it should immediately reinstate in its vocabulary. The OED notes that "pled", formerly only American usage, has become Scottish dialect – but it's not English.
Susan Loppert,
London

pointe (ballet); **on pointe**, not on point or en pointe

point-to-point

Pokemon no accents

Polari

A form of language used mostly by gay men and lesbians, derived in part from slang used by sailors, actors and prostitutes and popularised in the 1960s BBC radio comedy Round the Horne by the characters Julian and Sandy. Example: "Vada the dolly eke on the bona omee ajax" (Look at the gorgeous face on that nice man over there); "naff" is an example of Polari that has passed into more general use, as are "butch", "camp" and "dizzy"

pole position or **on pole** means starting from the front row in a motor race, so be careful if using metaphorically

police forces Metropolitan police (the Met after first mention), West Midlands police, New York police department (NYPD at second mention), etc; but note Police Service of Northern Ireland

police ranks PC on all references to police constable (never WPC), other ranks full out and initial cap at first reference; in leading articles abbreviation plus surname: Sgt Campbell, DC, Insp, Ch Insp, Det Supt, Ch Supt, Cmdr, etc (or just Mr, Ms or Mrs) otherwise just surname

police units lc: anti-terrorist branch, flying squad, fraud squad, special branch, vice squad

politburo

political correctness a term to be avoided on the grounds that it is, in Polly Toynbee's words, "an empty rightwing smear designed only to elevate its user"

political parties lc for word "party"; abbreviate if necessary (for example in parliamentary reporting) as C, Lab, Lib Dem (two words), SNP (Scottish National party, not "Scottish Nationalist party"), Plaid Cymru, SDLP (Social Democratic and Labour party), SF (Sinn Féin), UUP (Ulster Unionist party), DUP (Democratic Unionist party), Ukip (UK Independence party)

poncey not poncy

pop art

Pope, the but **papacy, pontiff**; normally no need to give his name in full

poppadom

Portakabin, Portaloo TM; say portable building, portable toilets

Porthmadog not Portmadoc

portland cement, portland stone

Port of London authority PLA on second mention

postal workers not postmen

postcode

Postcomm UK postal services regulator; its full name (which you do not need to use) is Postal Services Commission

postgraduate

Post-it TM

postmodern, postmodernist

postmortem

Post Office cap up the organisation, but you buy stamps in a **post office** or **sub-post office**

postwar

Potters Bar

PoW abbreviation for prisoner of war

Powergen

powerpop one word; musical genre defined by nostalgia for the 60s, in the form of chiming electric guitars and vocal harmonies. Its proponents often profess to being inspired by the Beatles and the Byrds, but are never as good as either

practice noun; **practise** verb

practising homosexual

Do not use this expression, or the equally grotesque "active homosexual"; where it is necessary to discuss someone's sex life, for example a story about gay clergy, it is possible to use other expressions, eg the Anglican church demands celibacy from gay clergy but permits the laity to have sexually active relationships

pre- redundant in such newly fashionable words as pre-booked, pre-reserved, pre-ordered, and even pre-rehearsed

precis singular and plural

predilection not predeliction

pre-eminent

prefab, prefabricated

premier only when constitutionally correct (eg leaders of Australian states or Canadian provinces), therefore not for Britain – do not use in headlines for British prime minister; the Chinese traditionally give their prime minister the title of premier, eg Premier Wen Jiabao

premiere no accent

Premier League (no longer FA Premier League or Premiership) in England; in Scotland, it was briefly the Premierleague, now the **Scottish Premier League** or more commonly **SPL**

premises of buildings and logic

premium bonds

prenuptial or (if you must) **prenup**

prepositions

Appeal against, protest against/over/at, not "appealed the sentence", "protested the verdict", etc.

Schoolchildren used to be told (by English teachers unduly influenced by Latin) that it was ungrammatical to end sentences with a preposition, a fallacy satirised by Churchill's "this is the sort of English up with which I will not put" and HW Fowler's "What did you bring me that book to be read to out of for?"

Take care after phrases following "to": the subheading "to we Conservatives, Labour looks as if it's heading back to the old horrors of the winter of discontent" drew numerous protests from readers pointing out that it should have been "to us Conservatives ... " (The mistake was ours, not the shadow cabinet minister who wrote the piece)

prepubescent

pre-Raphaelite

presently means soon, not at present

president lc except in title: President Bush, but George Bush, the US president

press, the singular: the British press is a shining example to the rest of the world

Press Complaints Commission PCC on second mention

Press Gazette formerly UK Press Gazette

pressured/pressurised use put pressure on or pressed to mean apply pressure, ie not "the Baggies pressured [or pressurised] the Wolves defence"

prestigious having prestige: nothing wrong with this, despite what wise old subeditors used to tell us

Pret a Manger food; **pret a porter** fashion

preteen

pretext by its nature false, so while it may or may not be true that Tony Blair went to war on a pretext, it is tautologous to say he did so on a false one

prevaricate "to speak or act falsely with intent to deceive" (Collins); often confused with **procrastinate**, to put something off

preventive not preventative

prewar

PricewaterhouseCoopers or **PWC**; note that PwC Consulting has become **Monday**

prima donna plural **prima donnas**

prima facie not italicised

primary care trusts lc, eg Southwark primary care trust

primate another word for archbishop; Primate of All England: Archbishop of Canterbury; Primate of England: Archbishop of York; but "the primate" on second reference

primates higher members of the order Primates, essentially apes and humans

prime minister write "Gordon Brown, the prime minister, said ... " not "prime minister Gordon Brown said ... "; never use the American English style "prime minister Brown"

primitive do not use to describe tribal people *see stone age*

Prince of Wales at first mention; thereafter Prince Charles or the prince

Prince's Trust

principal first in importance; **principle** standard of conduct

principality do not use to describe Wales

prise apart, open (not prize)

prison officer not warder, a term that the Prison Officers' Association regards as "degrading, insulting and historically inaccurate" (the Home Office changed it from warder in 1922)

Prison Service but **immigration service** lc (it is properly called the Immigration and Nationality Directorate)

private finance initiative PFI on second mention

privy council but **privy counsellor**

prize Booker prize, Nobel prize, Whitbread prize, etc *see awards*

prizefighter, prizewinner but **prize money**

proactive do not use this hideous jargon word with a hyphen. Or without one

probe a dental implement, not an inquiry or investigation

pro-choice not pro-abortion

procrastinate to delay or defer; often confused with **prevaricate**

procurator fiscal Scottish public prosecutor; the Crown Office and Procurator Fiscal Service (COPFS), in Scotland, more wide-ranging than the Crown Prosecution Service in England and Wales, is responsible for the prosecution of crime, investigation of sudden or suspicious deaths, and investigation of complaints against the police

prodigal wasteful or extravagant, not a returned wanderer; the confusion arises from the biblical parable of the prodigal son. A very common mistake

profile a noun, not a verb

program (computer); otherwise **programme**

prohibition lc for US prohibition

pro-life do not use to mean **anti-abortion**

Proms concerts; **proms** seafronts

prone face down; **supine** face up

proofreader, proofreading

propeller

prophecy noun; **prophesy** verb

pros and cons

protege male and female, no accents

protest against, over or **about** not, for example, "protest the election result", which has appeared on our front page

protester not protestor

proved/proven beware the creeping "proven", featuring (mispronounced) in every other TV ad; proven is not the normal past tense of prove, but a term in Scottish law ("not proven") and in certain English idioms, eg "proven record"

province avoid using this term to refer to Northern Ireland, described as "ugly and erroneous" by a reader

proviso plural **provisos**

Ps and Qs

public schools are actually **private schools**, so that is what we should call them

publicly not publically

public-private partnership PPP on second mention

Public Record Office merged with the Historical Manuscripts Commission in 2003 to form the **National Archives**

Puffa TM; say **padded** or **quilted jacket**

pundit self-appointed expert

purchase as a noun, perhaps, but use **buy** as a verb

put athletics; **putt** golf

Pwllheli

pygmy plural **pygmies**, lc except for members of Equatorial African ethnic group

pyjamas

pyrrhic victory

In an article in the Guardian on May 12 2007 entitled "Our 50 favourite campsites" the following was stated: "Toilets etc. Large toilet block and separate shower block. Portaloos in peak season."

I am writing to point out that "Portaloo" is a registered Trade Mark which may only be used to describe buildings manufactured by this Company. In order to protect our rights to the exclusive use of the Mark, we must take active steps to discourage its use as a generic term, and would ask that the attention of your staff be drawn to this letter and they be asked to use the designation "Portaloo" only in reference to the toilet units of this Company.

It is clearly not practicable for you to check whether all reports you receive mentioning "Portaloo" are in fact, referring to genuine Portaloo toilet units. In view of this, may I ask that, in any future cases of this kind, you use the term "portable toilets" or similar, there can then be no possibility of error.

I do assure you that this is of considerable importance to us and would, therefore, be most grateful for your cooperation in this matter.

Yours faithfully,

Dick Ellershaw, Trade Marks Officer, Portakabin Limited

"There's nothing to it
[subediting], really ... it's just a
matter of checking the facts and
the spelling, crossing out the first
sentence, and removing any
attempts at jokes."
**Michael Frayn, Towards the
End of the Morning**

Qq

Qantas

qat not kat or khat

QC use without comma, eg Cherie Booth QC

QE2, QM2 liners

QinetiQ arms company

Qom holy city in Iran

Qualifications and Curriculum Authority QCA after first mention

quango short for quasi-autonomous non-governmental organisation, but no need to spell out

quantum jump, quantum leap in any area other than physics, a cliche best avoided (unless you are referring to the cult 70s band Quantum Jump or the cult 90s TV series Quantum Leap)

quarterdeck, quartermaster

Québécois not Quebeckers

Queen, the if it is necessary to say so, she is Her Majesty or HM, never HRH

Queen's birthday honours list

Queen's Club in London

Queens' College, Cambridge

Queen's College, Oxford its official name is The Queen's College (named in honour of Queen Philippa in 1341)

Queen's Park tube station has an apostrophe

Queen's Park Scotland's oldest football club, winners of the Scottish Cup 10 times in the 19th century and twice runners-up in the FA Cup

Queens Park Rangers (no apostrophe) English football club

Queen's speech

Queen's University Belfast

queueing not queuing

quicklime, quicksand, quicksilver

quixotic

quiz a suspect is questioned, not quizzed (however tempting for headline purposes)

quizshow

Quorn TM

Why do your journalists persist in giving credence to pompous jargon coined by New Labour apparatchiks? I'm talking about the latest entry into the lexicon of politico-military gobbledegook: "drawdown". I always thought this was an accounting phrase relating to the debiting of moneys from an agreed budget. It now appears to have been redefined as a proxy for "phased withdrawal". I understand why the government might wish to obfuscate the fact of impending retreat by cloaking it in obscure terminology. What I don't understand is why journalists play along with this game.
Richard Lloyd, Oxted, Surrey

quotation marks

Use double quotes at the start and end of a quoted section, with single quotes for quoted words within that section. Place full points and commas inside the quotes for a complete quoted sentence; otherwise the point comes outside – "Anna said: 'Your style guide needs updating,' and I said: 'I agree.' "

but: "Anna said updating the guide was 'a difficult and time-consuming task'."

When beginning a quote with a sentence fragment that is followed by a full sentence, punctuate according to the final part of the quote, eg The minister called the allegations "blatant lies. But in a position such as mine, it is only to be expected."

Headlines and standfirsts (sparingly), captions and display quotes all take single quote marks.

For parentheses in direct quotes, use square brackets

quotes

Take care with direct speech: our readers should be confident that words appearing in quotation marks accurately represent the actual words uttered by the speaker, though ums and ahems can be removed and bad grammar improved. If you aren't sure of the exact wording, use indirect speech.

Where a lot of material has been left out, start off a new quote with "He added: ... ", or signify this with an ellipsis.

Take particular care when extracting from printed material, for example a minister's resignation letter.

Introduce the speaker from the beginning, or after the first sentence: it is confusing and frustrating to read several sentences or even paragraphs of a quote before finding out who is saying it.

Stories peppered with separately quoted words and short phrases are extremely irritating to the reader, and make it look as if we did not manage to catch the speaker's words properly. So when we reported that "the business community was accused of 'cynicism' in the fight against climate change yesterday" and "journalists said that the possible sale of the paper was 'dangerous' for their editorial independence," there is no need to quote the words cynicism and dangerous.

From the editor:

If a reader reads something in direct quotation marks in the Guardian he/she is entitled to believe that the reporter can vouch directly for the accuracy of the quote.

Copying quotes out of other newspapers without any form of attribution is simply bad journalism, never mind legally risky. If, where there are no libel issues, you're going to repeat quotes, then always say where they came from. It won't be much help in a legal action, but at least the reader can evaluate the reliability of the source. A quote in the Sunday Sport may – who knows – count for less than one from the Wall Street Journal.

If we're taking quotes from the radio or television it is our general policy to include an attribution. This matters less if it is a pooled interview or news conference that happens to be covered by, say, the BBC or Sky. If the quote comes from an exclusive interview on a radio or TV programme (eg, Today, Channel 4 News or Newsnight) we should always include an attribution

Qur'an holy book of Islam (not Koran); regarded as the word of God, having been recited by the prophet Muhammad, so in the eyes of Muslims it is wrong to suggest that the prophet "wrote" the Qur'an

Qureia, Ahmed Palestinian politician, popularly known as Abu Ala (which means "father of Ala" – it is not a nom de guerre); he was prime minister of the Palestinian Authority until Fatah was defeated by Hamas in the parliamentary elections

Rr

"It will be proved to thy face that thou hast men about thee that usually talk of a noun and a verb, and such abominable words as no Christian ear can endure to hear."

William Shakespeare, Henry VI Part 2

race card as in "play the race card", something of a cliche, especially at election times when someone is certain to be accused of this

racehorses race at a **racecourse** or **racetrack** and are listed in a **racecard**

racial terminology

Do not use ethnic to mean black or Asian people. In a British sense, they are an ethnic minority; in a world sense, of course, white people are an ethnic minority.

Just as in the Balkans or anywhere else, internal African peoples should, where possible, be called ethnic groups or communities rather than "tribes".

Avoid the word "immigrant", which is very offensive to many black and Asian people, not only because it is often incorrectly used to describe people who were born in Britain, but also because it has been used negatively for so many years that it carries imagery of "flooding", "swamping", "bogus", "scroungers", etc.

The words black and Asian should not be used as nouns, but as adjectives: black people rather than "blacks", an Asian woman rather than "an Asian", etc.

Say African-Caribbean rather than Afro-Caribbean

rack one's brains for something

rack and ruin

racked by guilt, with pain, not wracked

rackets not racquets, except in club titles

Rada Royal Academy of Dramatic Art; normally no need to spell out

Radio 1, Radio 2, Radio 3, Radio 4, Five Live, 6 Music, BBC7

radiographer takes x-rays; **radiologist** reads them

Radio Telifís Éireann Irish public broadcasting corporation

radius plural **radii**

raft something you float on; do not say "a raft of measures", which has very rapidly become a cliche (particularly in political reporting)

Raid redundant array of independent disks (data storage)

railway station train station is now acceptable

Rainbows for girls from five (four in Northern Ireland) to seven, at which point they may become Brownies

raincoat, rainfall, rainproof

Ramadan month of fasting for Muslims

Ramsay, Gordon ex-footballing chef but note that England's World Cup-winning manager in 1966 was **Alf Ramsey**

Ramsey Street where Neighbours become good friends

R&B

Range Rover no hyphen

Rangers not Glasgow Rangers

rarefy, rarefied

rateable

Rawlplug TM

Ray-Ban TM; it's OK to call them **Ray-Bans**

re or re-?

Use re- (with hyphen) when followed by the vowels e or u (not pronounced as "yu"): eg re-entry, re-examine, re-urge.

Use re (no hyphen) when followed by the vowels a, i, o or u (pronounced as "yu"), or any consonant: eg rearm, rearrange, reassemble, reiterate, reorder, reread, reuse, rebuild, reconsider.

Exceptions (where confusion with another word would arise): re-cover/recover, re-form/reform, re-creation/recreation, re-sign/resign

realpolitik lc, no italics

rear admiral Rear Admiral Horatio Hornblower at first mention, thereafter Adm Hornblower

received pronunciation (RP) a traditionally prestigious accent, associated with public schools and used by an estimated 3% of the population of England, also known as BBC English, Oxford English or the Queen's English; nothing to do with Standard English, which includes written as well as spoken language and can be (indeed, normally is) spoken with a regional accent

recent avoid: if the date is relevant, use it

redbrick university; the original six were Birmingham, Bristol, Leeds, Liverpool, Manchester and Sheffield

Red Crescent, Red Cross

referendum plural **referendums**

reforestation not reafforestation

re-form to form again

reform to change for the better; we should not take the initiators' use of the word at its face value, particularly in cases where the Guardian believes no improvement is likely

refute use this much-abused word only when an argument is disproved; otherwise **contest, deny, rebut**

regalia plural, of royalty; "royal regalia" is tautologous

regard with regard to not with regards to (but of course you give your regards to Broadway)

Regent's Park London

regime no accent

regional assemblies lc, eg East of England regional assembly; there are eight of them, representing English regions outside London, represented collectively by the English Regions Network

register office not registry office

registrar general

regrettable

reinstate

religious right

Renaissance, the

reopen

repellant noun; **repellent** adjective: you fight repellent insects with an insect repellant

repertoire an individual's range of skills or roles; **repertory** a selection of works that a theatre or dance company might perform

replaceable

report the Lawrence report, etc; use report on or inquiry into but not report into, ie not "a report into health problems"

reported speech

When a comment in the present tense is reported, use past tense: "She said: 'I **like** chocolate' " (present tense) becomes in reported speech "she said she **liked** chocolate" (not "she said she likes chocolate").

When a comment in the past tense is reported, use "had" (past perfect tense): "She said: 'I **ate** too much chocolate' " (past tense) becomes in reported speech "she said she **had eaten** too much chocolate" (not "she said she ate too much chocolate").

Once it has been established who is speaking, there is no need to keep attributing, so long as you stick to the past tense: "Alex said he would vote Labour. There was no alternative. It was the only truly progressive party," etc

republicans lc (except for US political party)

residents has a rather old-fashioned feel to it, especially in the deadly form "local residents"; on the whole, better to call them people

resistance, resistance fighters *see terrorism/terrorists*

restaurateur not restauranteur

résumé

retail prices index (RPI) prices not price, but normally no need to spell it out

Rethink formerly the National Schizophrenia Fellowship

reticent unwilling to speak; do not confuse with reluctant, as in this example from the paper: "Like most graduates of limited financial means, Louise Clark was reticent about handing over a huge wad of dosh"

Reuters

Rev, the at first mention, eg the Rev Joan Smith, subsequently Ms Smith in leading articles, otherwise just Smith; never say "Reverend Smith", "the Reverend Smith" or "Rev Smith"

reveille

Revelation last book in the New Testament: not Revelations, a very common error; its full name is The Revelation of St John the Divine

Revenue & Customs acceptable shorthand for HM Revenue and Customs, formed in 2005 from a merger of the Inland Revenue and HM Customs and Excise

rheumatoid arthritis do not call it rheumatism or arthritis, but it can be abbreviated to RA after first mention

Rhodes scholar

RIBA (not Riba) Royal Institute of British Architects

rice paddies tautologous, as padi is the Malay word for rice; so it should be paddy fields or simply paddies

Richter scale expresses the magnitude of an earthquake, but now largely superseded by the **moment magnitude scale**

rickety

ricochet, ricocheted, ricocheting

riffle to flick through a book, newspaper or magazine; often confused with **rifle**, to search or ransack and steal from, eg rifle goods from a shop

right wing, the right, rightwinger nouns; **rightwing** adjective

ringfence, ringtone

rivers lc, eg river Thames, Amazon river

riveted, riveting

RNIB Royal National Institute of Blind People (no longer "the Blind")

roadside

rob you rob a person or a bank, using force or the threat of violence; but you **steal** a car or a bag of money

Rock cap if referring to Gibraltar

rock'n'roll one word

role no accent

Rollerblade TM; say **inline skates**

rollercoaster one word

rollover (lottery)

Rolls-Royce

Romany noun, adjective; **Roma** plural

roofs plural of roof (not rooves, which has appeared in the paper)

ro-ro roll-on, roll-off ferry

Rorschach test psychological test based on the interpretation of inkblots

rottweiler

roué

roughshod

routeing/routing They are routeing buses through the city centre after the routing of the protesters

Rovers Return, the (no apostrophe) Coronation Street's pub

Royal Academy of Arts usually known as the **Royal Academy**

Royal Air Force or **RAF**

Royal Ballet

Royal Botanic Garden (Edinburgh); **Royal Botanic Gardens** (London), also known as **Kew Gardens** or simply **Kew**

Royal College of Surgeons the college or the royal college is preferable to the RCS on subsequent mention

royal commission

Royal Courts of Justice

royal family

Royal London hospital

Royal Mail

Royal Marines marines after first mention

Royal Navy or **the navy**

Royal Opera, Royal Opera House

royal parks

Royal Society of Arts RSA after first mention; its full name is Royal Society for the Encouragement of Arts, Manufactures and Commerce

RSPB, RSPCA do not normally need to be spelt out

Rubens, Peter Paul (1577-1640) Flemish painter

Rubicon

rugby league, rugby union

Rule, Britannia!

rupee Indian currency; **rupiah** Indonesian currency

russian roulette

I object to your use of the word "Christ" as an expletive in a large-print photo caption (Sharon Osbourne photograph). If you find it hard to understand that this can cause offence, it may help if you imagine using, in the same way, a name held dear by some other major world religion.

Andrew Waugh, Reading

Ss

"The practice of hinting by single letters those expletives with which profane and violent people are wont to garnish their discourse, strikes me as a proceeding which, however well meant, is weak and futile. I cannot tell what good it does – what feeling it spares – what horror it conceals."

Charlotte Brontë

Ss

Saatchi brothers Maurice (now Lord Saatchi) and Charles (the one with the gallery) founded M&C Saatchi in 1994 after leaving Saatchi & Saatchi, the advertising agency best known for the slogan "Labour isn't working" in the 1979 general election campaign

saccharin noun; **saccharine** adjective

sacrilegious not sacreligious

Sad seasonal affective disorder

Sadler's Wells

Safeway

Sahara no need to add "desert"

said normally preferable to added, commented, declared, pointed out, ejaculated, etc; you can avoid too many "saids", whether quoting someone or in reported speech, quite easily *see reported speech*

Sainsbury's for the stores; the company's name is **J Sainsbury plc**

Saint in running text should be spelt in full: Saint John, Saint Paul. For names of towns, churches, etc, abbreviate St (no point) eg St Mirren, St Stephen's church. In French placenames a hyphen is needed, eg St-Nazaire, Ste-Suzanne, Stes-Maries-de-la-Mer

St Andrews University no apostrophe

St Catharine's College, Cambridge

St Catherine's College, Oxford

St James Park home of Exeter City; **St James' Park** home of Newcastle United; **St James's Park** royal park in London

St John Ambulance not St John's and no longer "Brigade"

St Katharine Docks London

St Martin-in-the-Fields London

St Paul's Cathedral

Saint-Saëns, Camille (1835-1921) French composer

St Thomas' hospital in London; not St Thomas's

sake Japanese rice wine

saleable

Salonika not Thessaloniki

Salvation Army never the Sally Army

salvo plural **salvoes**

Samaritans the organisation has dropped "the" from its name

sambuca

Sana'a capital of Yemen

sanatorium (not sanitarium or sanitorium) plural **sanatoriums**

Sane mental illness charity

San Sebastián

San Serriffe island nation profiled in the Guardian on April 1 1977; **sans serif** typeface

San Siro stadium Milan

Sao Paulo Brazilian city, not Sao Paolo

Sars severe acute respiratory syndrome

Satan but **satanist, satanism**

satnav

Sats standard assessment tasks

SATs scholastic aptitude tests (in the US, where they are pronounced as individual letters)

Saumarez Smith, Charles the former director of the National Gallery

Savile, Sir Jimmy

Savile Club, Savile Row in London

Saville theatre in London, once owned by the Beatles' manager Brian Epstein and used for concerts in the 60s (Jimi Hendrix played there), is now the Odeon Covent Garden cinema

Scalextric

Scandinavia Denmark, Norway and Sweden; with the addition of Finland and Iceland, they constitute the **Nordic countries**

schadenfreude

scherzo plural **scherzos**

schizophrenia, schizophrenic use only in a medical context, never to mean "in two minds", contradictory, or erratic, which is wrong, as well as offensive to people diagnosed with this illness; schizophrenic should never be used as a noun

Schoenberg, Arnold (1874-1951) Austrian-born composer

schoolboy, schoolchildren, schoolgirl, schoolroom, schoolteacher

schools Alfred Salter primary school, Rotherhithe; King's school, Macclesfield; Eton college, etc

school years year 2, year 10, key stage 1, etc

Schröder, Gerhard former German chancellor

Schwarzenegger, Arnold Arnie acceptable in headlines

scientific measurements take care: "m"in scientific terms stands for "milli" (1mW is 1,000th of a watt), while "M" denotes "mega" (1MW is a million watts); in such circumstances it is wise not to bung in another "m" when you mean million, so write out, for example, 10 million C.

Some common measurements are: amps A, volts V, watts W, megawatts MW, milliwatts mW, joules J, kilojoules kJ

scientific names

In italics, with the first name (denoting the genus) capped, the second (denoting the species) lc; *Escherichia coli*, *Quercus robur*. The name can be shortened by using the first initial: *E coli*, *Q robur* (but we do not use a full point after the initial)

scientific terms some silly cliches you might wish to avoid: you would find it difficult to hesitate for a nanosecond (the shortest measurable human hesitation is probably about 250 million nanoseconds, or a quarter of a second); "astronomical sums" when talking about large sums of money is rather dated (the national debt surpassed the standard astronomical unit of 93 million [miles] 100 years ago)

261

scotch broth, scotch egg, scotch mist, scotch whisky but **Scotch argus** butterfly

ScotchTape TM; say **sticky tape**

Scotland

The following was written by a Scot who works for the Guardian and lives in London. Letters expressing similar sentiments come from across Britain (and, indeed, from around the world):

We don't carry much coverage of events in Scotland and to be honest, even as an expat, that suits me fine. But I do care very much that we acknowledge that Scotland is a separate nation and in many ways a separate country. It has different laws, education system (primary, higher and further), local government, national government, sport, school terms, weather, property market and selling system, bank holidays, right to roam, banks and money, churches, etc.

If we really want to be a national newspaper then we need to consider whether our stories apply only to England (and Wales) or Britain, or Scotland only. When we write about teachers' pay deals, we should point out that we mean teachers in England and Wales; Scottish teachers have separate pay and management structures and union. When we write about it being half term, we should remember that there's no such thing in Scotland. When we write about bank holiday sunshine/rain, we should remember that in Scotland the weather was probably different and it possibly wasn't even a bank holiday. When we write a back-page special on why the English cricket team is crap, we should be careful not to refer to it as "we" and "us". When the Scottish Cup final is played, we should perhaps consider devoting more than a few paragraphs at the foot of a page to Rangers winning their 100th major trophy (if it had been Manchester United we'd have had pages and pages with Bobby Charlton's all-time fantasy first XI and a dissertation on why English clubs are the best in Europe).

These daily oversights come across to a Scot as arrogance. They also undermine confidence in what the paper is telling the reader

Scotland Office not Scottish Office

Scott, Charles Prestwich (1846-1932) editor of the Manchester Guardian for 57 years and its owner from 1907 until his death (his uncle, John Edward Taylor, had founded the paper in 1821). Scott, who was editor when the first "Style-book of the Manchester Guardian" – forerunner of this publication – appeared in 1928, is most famous for his "comment is free, but facts are sacred" *see Appendix 3: CP Scott's 1921 essay on the centenary of the Manchester Guardian*

Scott, Sir George Gilbert (1811-78) architect who designed the Albert Memorial and Midland Grand hotel at St Pancras station

Scott, Sir Giles Gilbert (1880-1960), grandson of the above, responsible for red telephone boxes, Bankside power station (now Tate Modern), Waterloo bridge and the Anglican cathedral in Liverpool

Scottish Enterprise

Scottish executive

Scottish parliament members are **MSPs**

scottish terrier not scotch; once known as Aberdeen terrier

scouse, scouser

Scouts not "Boy Scouts" (in the UK, at least); the organisation is the Scout Association

Scoville scale system that measures the heat level of chillies

Scrabble TM

scratchcard, smartcard, swipecard

SCSI capped up even though generally pronounced "scuzzy"; it stands for small computer system interface

seaplane, seaport, seashore, seaside, seaweed

sea change, sea level, sea serpent, sea sickness

seal pups not "baby seals" for the same reason we don't call lambs "baby sheep"

Séamus, Seán note accents in Irish Gaelic; sean without a fada means old

Sea of Japan as generally known; but South Korea calls it the East Sea and North Korea the East Sea of Korea

seas, oceans uc, eg Black Sea, Caspian Sea, Pacific Ocean

seasons spring, summer, autumn, winter, all lc

second hand on a watch; but he bought it **secondhand**

secretary general

section 28 1988 law, widely regarded as homophobic, that said local authorities "shall not intentionally promote homosexuality or publish material with the intention of promoting homosexuality" or "promote the teaching in any maintained school of the acceptability of homosexuality as a pretended family relationship"; it was repealed in Scotland in 2000 and the rest of the UK in 2003

seize not sieze

self-control, self-defence, self-esteem, self-respect

Selfridges no apostrophe

Sellotape TM; say **sticky tape**

semicolon

Used correctly (which occasionally we do), the semicolon is a very elegant compromise between a full stop (too much) and a comma (not enough). This sentence, from a column by David McKie, illustrates beautifully how it's done: "Some reporters were brilliant; others were less so" *see colon*

semtex no longer necessary to cap this

Senate (US)

senior abbreviate to **Sr** not Sen or Snr, eg George Bush Sr

September 11, 9/11

The official death toll of the victims of the Islamist terrorists who hijacked four aircraft on September 11 2001 is 2,973. The figure includes aircraft passengers and crews, but not the 19 hijackers. Of this total, 2,749 died in the attacks on the twin towers of the World Trade Centre (1,541 have been identified from remains at Ground Zero), 184 were killed in the attack on the Pentagon, and 40 died when their plane crashed into a field near Shanksville, Pennsylvania.

The hijackers were: Fayez Ahmed, Mohamed Atta, Ahmed al-Ghamdi, Hamza al-Ghamdi, Saeed al-Ghamdi, Hani Hanjour, Nawaf al-Hazmi, Salem al-Hazmi, Ahmed al-Haznawi, Khalid al-Mihdhar, Majed Moqed, Ahmed al-Nami, Abdulaziz al-Omari, Marwan al-Shehhi, Mohannad al-Shehri, Wael al-Shehri, Waleed al-Shehri, Satam al-Suqami and Ziad Jarrah (though dozens of permutations of their names have appeared in the paper, we follow Reuters style as for most Arabic transliterations)

Serb noun; **Serbian** adjective: the Serbs ousted the Serbian dictator Slobodan Milosevic

sergeant major Sergeant Major Trevor Prescott, subsequently Sgt Maj (not RSM or CSM) Prescott in leading articles, otherwise just Prescott

Serious Fraud Office SFO on second mention

Serious Organised Crime Agency Soca after first mention

serjeant at arms

services, the (armed forces)

settler should be confined to those Israeli Jews living in settlements across the 1967 green line, ie in the occupied territories

set to

It is very tempting to use this, especially in headlines, when we think something is going to happen, but aren't all that sure. Try to resist this temptation. It is even less excusable when we do know that something is going to happen: one of our readers counted no fewer than 16 uses of the phrase in the paper in two days; in almost every case, the words could have been replaced with "will", or by simply leaving out the "set", eg "the packs are to come into force as part of the house-selling process".

The first readers' editor of the Guardian put it like this: "The expression 'set to', to mean about to, seems likely to ... is often used to refer to something that, though expected, is not absolutely certain to happen. It is a rascally expression that one of the readers who have learned to groan at the sight of it describes as an all-purpose term removing any precision of meaning from the sentence containing it"

Sex and the City not Sex in the City

sexing up

From the editor:

Guardian readers would rather we did give them the unvarnished truth – or our best stab at it. It seems obvious enough. But inside many journalists – this goes for desk editors as much as reporters – there is a little demon prompting us to make the story as strong and interesting as possible, if not more so. We drop a few excitable adjectives around the place. We overegg. We may even sex it up.

Strong stories are good. So are interesting stories. But straight, accurate stories are even better. Readers who stick with us over any length of time would far rather judge what we write by our own Richter scale of news judgments and values than feel that we're measuring ourselves against the competition. Every time we flam a story up we disappoint somebody – usually a reader who thought the Guardian was different.

We should be different. Of course we compete fiercely in the most competitive newspaper market in the world. Of course we want to sell as many copies as possible. We've all experienced peer pressure to write something as strongly as possible, if not more so. But our Scott Trust ownership relieves us of the necessity to drive remorselessly for circulation to the exclusion of all else. In other words, we don't need to sex things up, and we shouldn't

sex offenders register no apostrophe

sexuality

From a reader:

"Can I suggest your style guide should state that homosexual, gay, bisexual and heterosexual are primarily adjectives and that use of them as nouns should be avoided. It seems to me that this is both grammatically and politically preferable (politically because using them as nouns really does seem to define people by their sexuality). I would like to read that someone is 'homosexual', not 'a homosexual', or about 'gay people', not 'gays'. Lesbian is different as it is a noun that later began to be used adjectivally, not the other way round. As an example from Wednesday, the opening line 'Documents which showed that Lord Byron ... was a bisexual' rather than 'was bisexual' sounds both Daily Mail-esque and stylistically poor."

Sgt Pepper's Lonely Hearts Club Band 1967 album by a popular beat combo of the day; not Sergeant Pepper's Lonely Hearts Club Band

Shaanxi (capital Xi'an) and **Shanxi** (capital Taiyuan) are adjacent provinces in northern China

shakeout, shakeup

Shakespearean not Shakespearian

Shankill Road Belfast; not Shankhill

shantytown

shareholder

sharia law

sheepdog

sheikh

Shepherd Market Mayfair; **Shepherd's Bush** west London

Shetland or the **Shetland Isles** but never "the Shetlands"

Shia, Sunni two branches of Islam (note: not Shi'ite); plural **Shia Muslims** and **Sunni Muslims**, though Shias and Sunnis are fine if you are pushed for space

shiatsu massage; **shih-tzu** dog

ship not feminine: it ran aground, not she ran aground

shipbuilder, shipbuilding, shipmate, shipowner, shipyard

shoo-in not shoe-in

shoot-out

shopkeeper

Shoreham-by-Sea not Shoreham on Sea

Short money payment to opposition parties to help them carry out their parliamentary functions, named after Ted Short, the Labour leader of the house who introduced it in 1975

shrank not shrunk, except in the film title Honey, I Shrunk the Kids (and perhaps the occasional piece of wordplay based on it)

Siamese twins do not use: they are **conjoined twins**

sickbed, sicknote, sickroom but **sick pay**

sickie

side-effects

sidestreet

siege not seige

Siena Tuscan city; **sienna** pigment; **Sienna Miller** actor

silicon computer chips; **silicone** breast implants – we have been known to confuse the two, as in "Silicone Valley"

Silkin, Jon (1930-97) English poet, not to be confused with his cousin John Silkin (1923-87), a Labour cabinet minister, as was John's brother Sam Silkin (1918-88)

sim card (it stands for subscriber identity module)

since *see as or since?*

Singaporean names in three parts, eg Lee Kuan Yew

Singin' in the Rain not Singing

single quotes in headlines (but sparingly), standfirsts and captions

singles chart

sink past tense **sank**, past participle **sunk**: he sinks, he sank, he has sunk

Sinn Féin

siphon not syphon

sisyphean a futile or interminable task (Sisyphus had to spend eternity rolling a boulder up a hill)

six-day war

size family-size, fun-size

ski, skis, skier, skied, skiing

skilful not skillful

skipper usually only of a trawler

Sky+

slavery was not abolished in 1807, as we sometimes say: slavery in Britain became illegal in 1772, the slave trade in the British empire was abolished in 1807, but slavery remained in the colonies until the Slavery Abolition Act 1833

slither slide; **sliver** small piece

smallholding

Smith & Wesson

Smithsonian Institution not Institute

snowplough

so-called overused: as a reader pointed out when we used the term "so-called friendly fire", the expression is "obviously ironic and really doesn't need such ham-fisted pointing out"

socialism, socialist lc unless name of a party, eg Socialist Workers party

social security benefits all lc, income support, working tax credit, etc

sod's law *see Murphy's law*

Sofía queen of Spain

soi-disant means self-styled, not so-called; both phrases should be used sparingly

soiree

solar system *see planets*

solicitor general

Solzhenitsyn, Aleksandr Russian novelist

some do not use before a figure: if you are not sure, about or approximately are better, and if you are, it sounds daft: "some 12 people have died from wasp stings this year alone" was a particularly silly example that found its way into the paper

Sotheby's

soundbite

sources

Guardian journalists should use anonymous sources sparingly. We should – except in exceptional circumstances – avoid anonymous pejorative quotes. We should avoid misrepresenting the nature and number of sources, and we should do our best to give readers some clue as to the authority with which they speak. We should never, ever, betray a source *see Appendix 2: the editor's guidelines on the identification of sources*

south south London, south-west England, the south-east, south Wales, etc

Southbank Centre on the **South Bank** in London; **South Bank University**

southern hemisphere

south pole

Southport Visiter newspaper, not to be confused with the **Visitor,** Morecambe

spacehopper one word, no hyphen

spaghetti western

Doesn't the entry for stalactites rather miss an opportunity? "StalaCtites Cling tightly to the Ceiling; stalaGmites Grow mightily from the Ground."

Bob Malcolm,
Kimpton Bottom,
Hertfordshire

Spanish names and accents

Be aware that the surname is normally the second-to-last name, not the last, which is the mother's maiden name, eg the writer Federico García Lorca – known as García in Spain rather than Lorca – should be García Lorca on second mention. Note also that the female name Consuelo ends with an "o" not an "a".

In Spanish the natural stress of a word generally occurs on the second-to-last syllable. Words that deviate from this norm must carry a written accent mark, known as the *acento ortográfico*, to indicate where the stress falls. A guide to accents follows. If in doubt do an internet search (try the word with and without an accent) and look for reputable Spanish language sites, eg big newspapers.

Surnames ending -ez take an accent over the penultimate vowel, eg Benítez, Fernández, Giménez, Gómez, González, Gutiérrez, Hernández, Jiménez, López, Márquez, Martínez, Núñez, Ordóñez, Pérez, Quiñónez, Ramírez, Rodríguez, Sáez, Vásquez, Vázquez, Velázquez. Exception: Alvarez; note also that names ending -es do not take the accent, eg Martines, Rodrigues.

Other surnames Aristízabal, Beltrán, Cáceres, Calderón, Cañizares, Chevantón, Couñago, Cúper, Dalí, De la Peña, Díaz, Forlán, García, Gaudí, Miró, Muñoz, Olazábal, Pavón, Sáenz, Sáinz, Valdés, Valerón, Verón.

Forenames Adán, Alán, Andrés, César, Darío, Elías, Fabián, Ginés, Héctor, Hernán, Iñaki, Inés, Iván, Jesús, Joaquín, José, Lucía, María, Martín, Matías, Máximo, Míchel, Raúl, Ramón, Róger, Rubén, Sebastián, Víctor. The forenames Ana, Angel, Alfredo, Alvaro, Cristina, Diego, Domingo, Emilio, Ernesto, Federico, Fernando, Ignacio, Jorge, Juan, Julio, Luis, Marta, Mario, Miguel, Pablo and Pedro do not usually take accents.

Placenames Asunción, Bogotá, Cádiz, Catalonia, Córdoba, La Coruña, Guantánamo Bay, Guipúzcoa, Jaén, Jérez, León, Medellín, Potosí, San Sebastián, Valparaíso.

Sports teams, etc América, Atlético, El Barça (FC Barcelona), Bernabéu, Bolívar, Cerro Porteño, Deportivo La Coruña, Huracán, Málaga, Peñarol.

Note: Spanish is an official language in Argentina, Bolivia, Chile, Colombia, Costa Rica, Cuba, Dominican Republic, Ecuador, El Salvador, Equatorial Guinea, Guatemala, Honduras, Mexico, Nicaragua, Panama, Paraguay, Peru, Puerto Rico, Spain, Uruguay and Venezuela

Spanish practices, Spanish customs old Fleet Street expressions to be avoided

span of years 2007-10; but between 2007 and 2010, not "between 2007-10"

spare-part surgery avoid this term

spark overused in headlines of the "rates rise sparks fury" variety

spastic do not use

Speaker, the (Commons) but **deputy speaker** (of whom there are several)

special often redundant

special branch

Special Immigration Appeals Commission Siac or "the commission" on second mention

spellchecker if you use one, read through your work afterwards: a graphic on our front page was rendered nonsensical when a spellcheck turned the species *Aquila adalberti* into "alleyway adalberti", while *Prunella modularis* became "pronely modularise"; also note that most use American English spellings

spelled/spelt she spelled it out for him: "the word is spelt like this"

Spice Girls Victoria Beckham was Posh Spice; Melanie Brown was Scary Spice; Emma Bunton was Baby Spice; Melanie Chisholm was Sporty Spice; Geri Halliwell was Ginger Spice

spicy not spicey

Spider-Man but **Batman, Superman**

spin doctor

spinster avoid this old-fashioned term, which has acquired a pejorative tone; say, if relevant, that someone is an unmarried woman

spiral, spiralling prices (and other things) can spiral down as well as up; try a less cliched word that doesn't suggest a circular movement

split infinitives

"The English-speaking world may be divided into (1) those who neither know nor care what a split infinitive is; (2) those who do not know, but care very much; (3) those who know and condemn; (4) those who know and distinguish. Those who neither know nor care are the vast majority, and are happy folk, to be envied."
(HW Fowler, Modern English Usage, 1926)

It is perfectly acceptable, and often desirable, to sensibly split infinitives – "to boldly go" is an elegant and effective phrase – and stubbornly to resist doing so can sound pompous and awkward ("the economic precipice on which they claim perpetually to be poised") or ambiguous: "he even offered personally to guarantee the loan that the Clintons needed to buy their house " raises the question of whether the offer, or the guarantee, was personal.

George Bernard Shaw got it about right after an editor tinkered with his infinitives: "I don't care if he is made to go quickly, or to quickly go – but go he must!"

275

spoiled/spoilt she spoiled her son: in fact he was a spoilt brat

spokesman, spokeswoman if possible attribute a quote to the organisation, eg "The AA said … ", but if necessary say spokesman or spokeswoman rather than spokesperson

sponsorship

Try to avoid: we are under no obligation to carry sponsors' names. So London Marathon, not Flora London Marathon, etc. When a competition is named after a sponsor, it is unavoidable: C&G Trophy, etc; however, if the Guardian sponsors an event, we should say so

spoonful plural **spoonfuls** not spoonsful

spring

square brackets use for interpolated words in quotations, eg Maggie May said: "David [Cameron] has my full support"

square metres not the same as metres squared: eg 300m squared is 90,000 sq m, which is very different to 300 sq m; we often get this wrong

Square Mile rather old-fashioned term for City of London

squaw regarded as offensive: do not use

stadium plural **stadiums**

staff are plural

stalactites cling from the ceiling; **stalagmites** grow from the ground

stalemate in chess, a stalemate is the end of the game, and cannot be broken or resolved; **deadlock** or **impasse** are more suitable for metaphorical use

stamp not stomp

Stansted

Starck, Philippe French designer

Starkey, Zak (not Zac) son of Ringo Starr; plays drums for the Who

statehouse office of the state governor in the US; one word except in New Jersey where it is the state house

state of the union address

stationary not moving; **stationery** writing materials

STD or **STI**? STI (sexually transmitted infection) is a broader term than STD (sexually transmitted disease): you can have the infection without feeling ill or displaying any symptoms

steadfast

steamboat, steamhammer, steamship

steam engine

sten gun

stepchange avoid, unless you are quoting someone; **change** is perfectly adequate

stepfamily, stepfather, stepmother, etc, but **step-parents**

sterling the pound; sterling qualities

I had a horrible shock when I saw the dreaded word "stepchange" in the Guardian ... Please, please don't allow this frightful management-speak monstrosity house room. It's a blighted creature, and should be banished to survive as best it can in the world of government press releases, management consultants and bullshit bingo cards.
**Fran Acheson,
London**

Stetson hat

sticky-back plastic

stiletto plural **stilettos**

still life plural **still lifes**

stilton cheese

stimulus plural **stimuli**

stock exchange, London Stock Exchange

stock in trade

stockmarket

stone age

As recently as 2006, we used the phrase "stone age tribe" in a headline to describe the inhabitants of the Andaman Islands. The charity Survival says: "'Stone age' and 'primitive' have been used to describe tribal people since the colonial era, reinforcing the idea that they have not changed over time and that they are backward. This idea is both incorrect and very dangerous: incorrect because all societies adapt and change, and dangerous because it is often used to justify the persecution or forced 'development' of tribal people"

stony broke, stony-hearted not stoney

storey plural **storeys** (buildings)

straightforward

straitjacket

strait-laced

strait of Dover, strait of Gibraltar, strait of Hormuz not "straits"

Strategic Rail Authority SRA on second mention

Stratford-on-Avon district council and parliamentary seat, although most other local organisations, such as the Royal Shakespeare Company, call this Warwickshire town Stratford-upon-Avon

stratum plural **strata**

Street-Porter, Janet

streetwise

stretchered off do not use; say **carried off on a stretcher**

strippergram

stumbling block

Sturm und Drang German literary movement

stylebook but **style guide**

Subbuteo table football game where players "flick to kick", named after the bird of prey *Falco subbuteo* (the hobby)

subcommittee, subcontinent, subeditor, sublet, sublieutenant, subplot, subsection

subjunctive

The author Somerset Maugham noted more than 50 years ago: "The subjunctive mood is in its death throes, and the best thing to do is put it out of its misery as soon as possible." Would that that were so.

Most commonly, it is a third person singular form of the verb expressing hypothesis, typically something demanded, proposed, imagined: he demanded that she resign at once, I propose that she be sacked, she insisted Jane sit down.

The subjunctive is particularly common in American English and in formal or poetic contexts: If I were a rich man, etc. It can sound hyper-correct or pretentious, so use common sense; Fowler notes that it is "seldom obligatory"

submachine gun

submarines are boats, not ships

subpoena, subpoenaed

sub-Saharan

suchlike

Sudan not the Sudan

sudoku

suffer little children nothing to do with suffering, this frequently misquoted or misunderstood phrase was used by Christ (Luke 18:16) to mean "allow the little children to come to me"; it is also the title of a song about the Moors murders on the first Smiths album

suicide

Say that someone killed him or herself rather than "committed suicide"; suicide has not been a crime in the UK for many years and this old-fashioned term can cause unnecessary further distress to families who have been bereaved in this way.

Journalists should exercise particular care in reporting suicide or issues involving suicide, bearing in mind the risk of encouraging others. This applies to presentation, including the use of pictures, and to describing the method of suicide. Any substances should be referred to in general rather than specific terms. When appropriate, a helpline number (eg Samaritans) should be given. The feelings of relatives should also be carefully considered

summer

summer solstice the longest day of the year, but not the same as Midsummer Day (although we often seem to assume it is)

Super Bowl

supercasino

supermarkets Marks & Spencer or M&S, Morrisons, Safeway, Sainsbury's, Tesco (no wonder people get confused about apostrophes)

supermodel every new face who makes a name for herself these days is labelled a supermodel; model is normally sufficient

supersede not supercede

supply, supply days (parliament)

supreme court

Sure Start

surge prefer rise or increase, if that is the meaning; but surge is preferable to "upsurge"

surrealism

svengali (lc) although named after the sinister Svengali in George du Maurier's 1894 novel Trilby

swap not swop

swat flies; **swot** books

swath, swaths broad strip, eg cut a wide swath; **swathe, swathes** baby clothes, bandage, wrappings

swearwords

We are more liberal than any other newspaper, using language that our competitors would not. But even some Guardian readers who agree with Lenny Bruce that "take away the right to say fuck and you take away the right to say fuck the government" might feel that we sometimes use such words unnecessarily.

The editor's guidelines are as follows:

First, remember the reader, and respect demands that we should not casually use words that are likely to offend.

Second, use such words only when absolutely necessary to the facts of a piece, or to portray a character in an article; there is almost never a case in which we need to use a swearword outside direct quotes.

Third, the stronger the swearword, the harder we ought to think about using it.

Finally, never use asterisks, which are just a cop-out (as elegantly put by Charlotte Brontë in the quotation at the beginning of this section)

swingeing

swinging 60s

synopsis plural **synopses**

syntax beware of ambiguous or incongruous sentence structure – the following appeared in a column in the paper: "This argument, says a middle-aged lady in a business suit called Marion, is just more London stuff … " (What were her other outfits called?)

synthesis, synthesise, synthesiser

Tt

"I will have none of your damned cutting and slashing ... You shan't make canticles out of my canto [Don Juan] ... I will not give way to all the cant of Christendom."

Lord Byron

T (not tee) as in it suited her to a T, he had it down to a T

tableau plural **tableaux**

table d'hote

tactics singular and plural

Taiwanese names like Hong Kong and Korean names, these are in two parts with a hyphen, eg Lee Teng-hui (Lee after first mention)

Tajikistan adjective **Tajik**

takeoff noun; **take off** verb

takeover

Takeover Panel

Taliban plural (it means "students")

talkshow

TalkSport although the radio station's brand is talkSPORT

Tamiflu not a vaccine for bird flu, as often described: it's an antibiotic used to treat it

tam o'shanter woollen cap

Tampax TM; say **tampon**

Tangier not Tangiers

Tannoy TM; say **public address system** or just **PA**

taoiseach Irish prime minister (prime minister is also acceptable)

targeted, targeting

tariff

Tarmac a company; **tarmac** formerly used to make pavements, roads and runways (we now walk and drive on asphalt)

tarot cards

taskforce

Tate The original London gallery in Millbank, now known as **Tate Britain**, houses British art from the 16th century; **Tate Modern**, at Southwark, south London, **Tate Liverpool** and **Tate St Ives**, in Cornwall, all house modern art

Tavener, Sir John English composer of such works as The Protecting Veil (1988)

Taverner, John English composer (c1490-1545) of masses and other vocal works

tax avoidance is legal; **tax evasion** is illegal

taxi, taxiing of aircraft

Tbilisi capital of Georgia

teabag, teacup, teapot, teaspoon

team-mate

teams

Sports teams take plural verbs: Australia have won by an innings, Wednesday were relegated again, etc; but note that in a business context they are singular like other companies, eg Leeds United reported its biggest loss to date

teargas

Teasmade TM; say **teamaker**

Technicolor TM

teddy boy (1950s)

Teesside

teetotaller

Teflon TM; say **non-stick pan**

telephone numbers hyphenate after three- or four-figure area codes, but not five-figure area codes: 020-7278 2332, 0161-832 7200; 01892 456789, 01227 123456; treat mobile phone numbers as having five-figure area codes: 07911 654321

Teletubbies they are: **Tinky Winky** (purple); **Laa-Laa** (yellow); **Dipsy** (green); and **Po** (red)

television shows chatshow, gameshow, quizshow, talkshow

temazepam

temperatures thus: 30C (85F) – ie celsius, with fahrenheit in brackets on first mention; but be extremely wary (or don't bother) when converting temperature changes, eg an average temperature change of 2C was wrongly converted to 36F in an article about a heatwave (although a temperature of 2C is about the same as 36F, a temperature change of 2C corresponds to a change of about 4F)

Ten Commandments

tendinitis not tendonitis

Tenerife

tenses

We've Only Just **Begun** was playing on the radio. He **began** to drink; in fact he **drank** so much, he was **drunk** in no time at all. He **sank** into depression, knowing that all his hopes had been **sunk**. Finally, he **sneaked** away. Or perhaps **snuck** away (according to Steven Pinker, the most recent irregular verb to enter the language).
see burned, dreamed, drink, learned, sink, spelled, spoiled

Terfel, Bryn Welsh opera singer; please note he is a bass baritone, not a tenor

terrace houses not terraced

terracotta, terra firma

Terrence Higgins Trust

terrorism/terrorists

A terrorist act is directed against victims chosen either randomly or as symbols of what is being opposed (eg workers in the World Trade Centre, tourists in Bali, Spanish commuters). It is designed to create a state of terror in the minds of a particular group of people or the public as a whole for political or social ends. Although most terrorist acts are violent, you can be a terrorist without being overtly violent (eg poisoning a water supply or gassing people on the underground).

Does having a good cause make a difference? The UN says no: "Criminal acts calculated to provoke a state of terror in the general public are in any circumstances unjustifiable, whatever the considerations of a political, philosophical, ideological, racial, ethnic, religious or other nature that may be invoked to justify them."

Whatever one's political sympathies, suicide bombers, the 9/11 attackers and most paramilitary groups can all reasonably be regarded as terrorists (or at least groups some of whose members perpetrate terrorist acts).

Nonetheless we need to be very careful about using the term: it is still a subjective judgment – one person's terrorist may be another person's freedom fighter, and there are former "terrorists" holding elected office in many parts of the world. Some critics suggest that, for the Guardian, all terrorists are militants – unless their victims are British. Others may point to what they regard as "state terrorism".

Often, alternatives such as militants, radicals, separatists, etc, may be more appropriate and less controversial, but this is a difficult area: references to the "resistance", for example, imply more sympathy to a cause than calling such fighters "insurgents". The most important thing is that, in news reporting, we are not seen – because of the language we use – to be taking sides.

Note that the phrase "war on terror" should always appear in quotes, whether used by us or (more likely) quoting someone else

Tesco not Tesco's

Tessa tax-exempt special savings account, replaced by Isa

Test (cricket) the third Test, etc

Texan a person; the adjective is **Texas**: Texas Ranger, Texas oilwells, Texas tea, etc

textbook

that do not use automatically after the word "said", but it can be useful: you tend to read a sentence such as "he said nothing by way of an explanation would be forthcoming" as "he said nothing by way of an explanation" and then realise that it does not say that at all; "he said that nothing by way of an explanation would be forthcoming" is much clearer

that or which?

"that" defines, "which" gives extra information (often in a clause enclosed by commas):

This is the house that Jack built, but this house, which John built, is falling down;

The Guardian, which I read every day, is the paper that I admire above all others.

Note that in such examples the sentence remains grammatical without "that", but not without "which"

the

Leaving "the" out often reads like jargon: say the conference agreed to do something, not "conference agreed"; the government has to do, not "government has to"; the Super League (rugby), not "Super League".

Avoid "prime minister Gordon Brown" syndrome: do not use constructions such as "prime minister Gordon Brown said". Prominent figures can just be named, with their function at second mention: "Gordon Brown said last night" (first mention); "the prime minister said" (subsequent mentions). If it is thought necessary to explain who someone is, write "Bryan Robson, the Sheffield United manager, said" or "the Sheffield United manager, Bryan Robson, said". In such cases the commas around the name indicate there is only one person in the position, so write "the Tory leader, David Cameron, said" (only one person in the job), but "the former Tory prime minister John Major said" (there have been many).

lc for newspapers (the Guardian), magazines (the New Statesman), pubs (the Coach and Horses), bands (the Beatles, the Black Eyed Peas, the The), nicknames (the Hulk, the Red Baron), and sports grounds (the Oval).

uc for books (The Lord of the Rings), films (The Matrix), poems (The Waste Land), works of art (The Haywain), music (The Kick Inside), television shows (The West Wing), and placenames (The Hague)

Tt

theatre normally lc in name, eg Adelphi theatre, Crucible theatre (or just Adelphi, Crucible); initial cap if "Theatre" comes first, eg Theatre Royal, Stratford East

theatregoer

theirs no apostrophe

then the then prime minister, etc (no hyphen)

thermonuclear

Thermos TM; say **vacuum flask**

thinktank one word

Third Reich

third way

third world meaning not the west (first) or the Soviet Union (second), so today an outdated (as well as objectionable) term; use **developing countries** or **developing nations**

this and that

that was then, but this is now; this looks forward, that looks back: so the man showing his son and heir the lands lying in front of them says: "One day, son, all this will be yours." Then he points behind him to the house and says: "But that remains mine"

thoroughbred, thoroughgoing

threefold, threescore

three-line whip

thunderstorm

Tiananmen Square Beijing

Tianjin not Tientsin

tidal wave just what it says it is; **tsunami** huge wave caused by an underwater earthquake

tidewater

tikka masala

timebomb, timescale, timeshare

times 1am, 6.30pm, etc; 10 o'clock last night but 10pm yesterday; half past two, a quarter to three, 10 to 11, etc; for 24-hour clock, 00.47, 23.59; use noon, midday or midnight rather than 12am, 12pm

Timor-Leste formerly East Timor

tinfoil

Tipp-Ex TM; use **correction fluid** (not that many people do any more)

Telephone and fax numbers are frequently being given out in the form 0207 xxx xxxx. This is complete nonsense. The correct form is 020 7xxx xxxx. I have had enough of this cluelessness. Every published instance of an incorrect telephone number increases the number of people who do not correctly know their own numbers. As a company that reaches out to the public, you have a moral responsibility to set a good example.

Stewart Gordon, Loughborough

tipping point another example of jargon that has quickly become hackneyed through overuse

titbit not tidbit

titles

Do not italicise or put in quotes titles of books, films, TV programmes, paintings, songs, albums or anything else. Words in titles take initial caps except for a, an, and, at, for, from, in, of, the, to (except in initial position or after a colon): A Tale of Two Cities, Happy End of the World, Shakespeare in Love, Superman: The Early Years, War and Peace, Who Wants to Be a Millionaire?, etc. Exception: the Review *see italics*

T-junction

toby jug inexplicably capped up in the paper at least twice

to-do as in "what a to-do!"

told the Guardian we use this phrase too often: it should normally be replaced by "said" and reserved for occasions when it genuinely adds interest or authority to a story (if someone got an exclusive interview with, say, Osama bin Laden)

Tolkien, JRR (1892-1973) British author and philologist, notable for writing The Lord of the Rings and not spelling his name "Tolkein"

tomato plural **tomatoes**

tonnage measured in tons (units of volume), not tonnes (units of mass) – derived from the number of tuns (large barrels) a vessel could hold; registered tonnage is the total internal capacity of a vessel, displacement tonnage is its actual weight, equal to the weight of water it displaces

tonne not ton (with the above exception): the metric tonne is 1,000kg (2,204.62lb), the British ton is 2,240lb, and the US ton is 2,000lb; usually there is no need to convert

top 10, top 40 etc

top hat

Topman, Topshop

tornado plural **tornadoes** (storm); **Tornado** plural **Tornados** (aircraft)

tortuous a tortuous road is one that winds or twists

torturous a torturous experience is one that involves pain or suffering

Tory party

total avoid starting court stories with variations on the formula "three men were jailed for a total of 19 years", a statistic that conveys no meaningful information (in this case, they had been given sentences of nine, six and four years).

The only time this might be justified is when one person is given a series of life sentences, and "he was jailed for a total of 650 years" at least conveys how serious the crimes were

totalisator, the tote

totalled

touchdown

Toussaint, Allen US blues musician

Toussaint, Jean US jazz musician

Tt

Toussaint
L'Ouverture,
François
Dominique
– Treasury, the

guardian style

Toussaint L'Ouverture, François Dominique (1743-1803) leader of Haiti's slave revolt of 1791 and subsequent fight for independence, which was granted in 1801

town councillor, town hall

Townshend, Pete one of the two members of the Who who didn't die before he got old (the other is Roger Daltrey)

trademarks (TM)

Take care: use a generic alternative unless there is a very good reason not to, eg ballpoint pen, not biro (unless it really is a Biro, in which case it takes a cap B); say photocopy rather than Xerox, etc; you will save our lawyers, and those of Portakabin and various other companies, a lot of time and trouble

trade union, trade unionist, trades union council

tragic use with care, especially avoiding cliches such as "tragic accident"

transatlantic

Transnistria separatist region that declared its independence from Moldova in 1990, but has not been recognised by the international community; also known as **Trans-Dniester**

Transport for London TfL on second mention

Trans-Siberian railway

Travellers capped: they are recognised as an ethnic group under the Race Relations Act; but note **new age travellers** lc

Treasury, the (officially HM Treasury)

treaties lc, eg Geneva convention, treaty of Nice

Trekkers how to refer to Star Trek fans unless you want to make fun of them, in which case they are **Trekkies**

trenchcoat

tricolour French and Irish

trillion a thousand billion (1 followed by 12 noughts), abbreviate like this: $25tn

Trinity College, Cambridge not to be confused with **Trinity Hall, Cambridge**

Trinity College Dublin

trip-hop

Trips trade-related intellectual property rights

trooper soldier in a cavalry regiment; **trouper** member of a troupe, or dependable worker ("Guardian subeditors are real troupers")

trooping the colour (no "of")

tropic of cancer, tropic of capricorn

Troubles, the (Northern Ireland)

try to never "try and", eg "I will try to do something about this misuse of language"

tsar not czar

tsetse fly

T-shirt not tee-shirt

tsunami wave caused by an undersea earthquake; not a tidal wave

tube, the lc (London Underground is the name of the company); individual lines thus: Jubilee line, Northern line, etc; the underground

TUC Trades Union Congress, so TUC Congress is tautological; the reference should be to the **TUC conference**

Tupperware TM

turgid does not mean apathetic or sluggish – that's **torpid** – but swollen, congested, or (when used of language) pompous or bombastic

turkish delight

Turkmenistan adjective **Turkmen**; its citizens are **Turkmen**, singular **Turkman**

Turkomans (singular noun and adjective is **Turkoman**) are a formerly nomadic central Asian people who now form a minority in Iraq; they speak **Turkmen**

turned the subeditor turned stylebook guru, Amelia Hodsdon, said ... (no hyphens)

turnover noun; **turn over** verb

21st century but hyphenate if adjectival: "newspapers of the 21st century", "21st-century newspapers"

Twenty20 cricket

twofold

tying

Uu

"I believe more in the scissors
than I do in the pencil."
Truman Capote

Uu

uber no accent if you are saying something like uber-hip, but use the umlaut if you are quoting German

U-boat

Ucas Universities and Colleges Admissions Service, but no need to spell it out

Uighur, Uighurs the Uighur people, particularly of the Xinjiang region in China

UK or **Britain** in copy and headlines for the United Kingdom of Great Britain and Northern Ireland (but note Great Britain comprises just England, Scotland and Wales)

Ukraine no "the"; adjective **Ukrainian**

ukulele not ukelele

Ulster avoid if possible but acceptable in headlines to mean Northern Ireland, which in fact comprises six of the nine counties of the province of Ulster

Uluru formerly known as Ayers Rock

Umist the former University of Manchester Institute of Science and Technology merged with the University of Manchester in 2004

umlaut

In German placenames, ae, oe and ue should almost always be rendered ä, ö, ü. Family names, however, for the most part became petrified many years ago and there is no way of working out whether the -e form or the umlaut should be used; you just have to find out for each individual

UN

UN No need to spell out United Nations, even at first mention

UNAids

Unesco United Nations Educational, Scientific and Cultural Organisation; no need to spell it out

UN general assembly

UNHCR United Nations high commissioner for refugees; not commission (although the name stands for both the high commissioner and the refugee agency s/he fronts)

Unicef United Nations Children's Fund; no need to spell it out

UN secretary general

UN security council

unbiased

uncharted not unchartered

unchristian

uncooperative

underachieve, underact, underage, undercover, underdeveloped, undermanned, underprivileged, undersea, undersigned, undervalue, underweight

underestimate, understate take care that you don't mean overestimate or overstate (we often get this wrong)

underground, the but **London Underground** for name of company

under way not underway

uneducated "with no formal education" may be more appropriate

uninterested means not taking an interest and is not synonymous with disinterested, which means unbiased

union lc when debating the future of "the union" (England and Scotland)

union flag not union jack

unionists (Northern Ireland), lc except in the name of a party, eg Ulster Unionist party

unique one of a kind, so cannot be qualified as "absolutely unique", "very unique", etc

Unite the UK's biggest trade union, formed in 2007 by the merger between Amicus and the Transport and General Workers' Union

United Kingdom England, Wales, Scotland and Northern Ireland; no need to write in full: say Britain or the UK

United Reformed Church not United Reform Church, as pointed out on a wearisomely regular basis in the corrections column

universities cap up, eg Sheffield University, Johns Hopkins University, Free University of Berlin

University College London no comma; **UCL** after first mention

University of the Arts London comprises Camberwell College of Arts, Central Saint Martins College of Art and Design, Chelsea College of Art and Design, London College of Communication, London College of Fashion, and Wimbledon College of Art

You justifiably mourn the dilution in meaning of words such as disinterested, but what do you make of the Guardian's increasingly cavalier use of unique? The Taj Mahal, Shane Warne's bowling, the Mona Lisa – all might qualify as unique, but a small cardboard box for keeping pamphlets in? ("How to receive a unique free box for your speeches and CD", front page).
David Barford, Cardiff

Unknown Soldier tomb of the

unmistakable

until not "up until"

unveiled pictures are, as are cars sometimes, but these days almost everything seems to be – so the government "unveiled a raft of new policies" (two cliches and a redundant "new" in six words) or a company "unveiled record profits". There is nothing wrong with announcing, reporting, presenting or publishing. US profits may be "posted" but probably not British ones

upbeat, upfront, upgrade, upmarket, upstage, uptight but **upside down**

upcoming the coining and, even worse, use of such jargon words is likely to make many otherwise liberal, enlightened Guardian readers (and stylebook editors) wonder if there is not after all a case to bring back capital, or at least corporal, punishment for crimes against the English language; an editor once told his staff: "If I read upcoming in the Wall Street Journal again, I shall be downcoming and somebody will be outgoing"

upmarket, downmarket

up to date but in an up-to-date fashion

US for United States, not USA; no need to spell out, even at first mention; America is also acceptable *see America*

USAid

user-generated content

utopian

U-turn

Uzbekistan adjective **Uzbek**

Vv

"Substitute 'damn' every time
you're inclined to write 'very'.
Your editor will delete it and the
writing will be just as it should be."
Mark Twain

Vv

v (roman) for versus, not vs: England v Australia, Rushden & Diamonds v Sheffield Wednesday, state v private, etc

Vajpayee, Atal Bihari former prime minister of India

Val d'Isère

Valentine's Day

Valium TM; a brand of diazepam

valley lc, eg Thames valley, Ruhr valley, the Welsh valleys, valley girl

Valparaíso

Valuation Office Agency (VOA after first mention) an executive agency of HM Revenue & Customs, it compiles business rating and council tax valuation lists for England and Wales but not Scotland, where the job is done by the Scottish Assessors

ValuJet Atlanta-based budget airline now called **AirTran**

V&A abbreviation for Victoria and Albert Museum

Vanessa-Mae violinist (note hyphen)

Van Gogh, Vincent (1853-90) Dutch artist; note that as with other Dutch names it is Van Gogh when just the surname is used (a Van Gogh masterpiece) but van Gogh with the forename (a masterpiece by Vincent van Gogh)

Vanuatu formerly New Hebrides

vapour but **vaporise**

Vargas Llosa, Mario Peruvian writer and politician

Vaseline TM; call it **petroleum jelly**

VAT value added tax; no need to spell it out

Vaughan or **Vaughn**?
Frankie Vaughan
Johnny Vaughan
Michael Vaughan
Sarah Vaughan

Matthew Vaughn
Robert Vaughn
Vince Vaughn

VE Day May 8 1945; **VJ Day** August 15 1945

Vehicle Inspectorate

Velázquez, Diego (1599-1660) Spanish painter

Velcro TM

veld not veldt

venal open to bribery; **venial** easily forgiven

venetian blind

veranda not verandah

verdicts recorded by coroners; returned by inquest juries

Verkhovna Rada (supreme council) Ukraine's parliament

vermilion

verruca not verucca

verse *see poetry*

very usually very redundant

Vv

Vespa scooters; **Vesta** curries

veterinary

veto, vetoes, vetoed, vetoing

Viagra TM; the generic is **sildenafil citrate**

vicar a cleric of the Anglican church (which also has rectors and curates, etc), not of any other denomination.

A priest writes: "A vicar is a person who is the incumbent of a parish, and the term is a job description in the same way that editor is a job description. All editors are journalists but not all journalists are editors. In the same way, all vicars are priests, but not all priests are vicars. Some priests are chaplains; some (like me) are forensic social workers; some are retired; some are shopworkers; some are police officers"

vice-chair, vice-chancellor, vice-president

vice versa

vichyssoise

videotape noun and verb, although normally shorten to video or tape (the two are interchangeable – Did you video that programme? No, I taped something else)

vie, vying

Villa-Lobos, Heitor (1887-1959) Brazilian composer

virtuoso plural **virtuosos**

virus not the same as a bacterium, but we often confuse the two; if in doubt, consult the science desk

vis-a-vis

vocal cords not chords

Vodafone

voiceover

volcano plural **volcanos**

vortex plural **vortices**

You bundle together letters on resistant TB, malaria
and HIV under the heading of "Africa's killer
viruses". This is a mistake in nomenclature that the
Guardian frequently makes, calling all infections a
"virus". HIV is a virus, like measles and influenza;
TB is a bacterium, like MRSA and legionnaires'
disease, and malaria is caused by a protozoan, like
the common amoeba. These terms reflect profound
biological differences. If this is too difficult, may I
suggest the generic term – "bugs".

Dr Gavin Bullock, Winchester

Ww

"The web, then, or the pattern,
a web at once sensuous and
logical, an elegant and pregnant
texture: that is style, that is the
foundation of the art of
literature."

Robert Louis Stevenson

wacky not whacky

wagon not waggon

Wags wives and girlfriends (generally of footballers: the term was popularised during the 2006 World Cup); the singular is **Wag**. Now in danger of overuse, and arguably sexist – although variations include Habs (husbands and boyfriends); for a full list, see the Wikipedia entry

Wahhabism branch of Islam practised by followers of the teachings of Muhammad ibn Abd-al-Wahhab (1703-92)

wah-wah pedal

waive, waiver the relinquishing of a claim or right; **waver** to hesitate

wake "in the wake of" is overused; nothing wrong with "as a result of" or simply "after"

Wales avoid the word "principality"; not a unit of measurement ("50 times the size of Wales")

Wales Office not Welsh Office

walking stick

Walkman TM; plural **Walkmans** not Walkmen

Wallpaper* magazine (note asterisk)

Wall's ice-cream, sausages

Wal-Mart owner of Asda

Wap (wireless application protocol) phones

war crime, war dance, war game

warhead, warhorse, warlord, warpath, warship, wartime

"war on terror" always in quotes

wars

first world war, second world war (do not say "before the war" or
"after the war" when you mean the second world war)
hundred years war (it actually lasted 116 years, from 1337 to 1453)
war of Jenkins' ear (1739-48)
civil war (England), American civil war, Spanish civil war
Crimean/Boer/Korean/Vietnam war
six-day war
Gulf war (1991), Iraq war (2003)

washing-up liquid

washout

Was (Not Was) defunct US rock band

Waste Land, The poem by TS Eliot (not The Wasteland)

watchdog, watchmaker, watchword

**watercolour, watercourse, watermark, waterproof,
waterskiing, waterworks**

Waterford Wedgwood glass and china (not Wedgewood)

water polo

Waterstone's bookshop

Watford Gap a service area on the M1 in Northamptonshire,
named after a nearby village 80 miles north of London; nothing

to do with the Hertfordshire town of Watford, with which it is sometimes confused by lazy writers who think such phrases as "anyone north of the Watford Gap" a witty way to depict the unwashed northern hordes

wayzgoose traditional term for a printer's works outing

web, webpage, website, world wide web

web 2.0

Weee directive (note three Es) EU scheme to encourage recycling of waste electrical and electronic equipment

weight in kilograms with imperial conversion, eg 65kg (10st 2lb)

Weight Watchers TM

welch (not welsh) to fail to honour an obligation

Welch Regiment, Royal Welch Fusiliers

welfare state

wellbeing

well-known as with famous, if someone or something is well-known, it should not be necessary to say so

wellnigh

Welsh, Irvine Scottish author

Welsh assembly official name the National Assembly for Wales; members are AMs

welsh dresser

welsh rarebit

Welsh spellings (eg F for the V sound in English, DD for the TH sound): prefer Welsh spellings such as Caernarfon and Conwy to old-fashioned anglicised versions (Caernarvon, Conway) – although there are exceptions, such as Cardiff not Caerdydd

Wen Jiabao succeeded Zhu Rongji as Chinese premier (prime minister) in 2003; Wen at second mention (except in leading articles where he is Mr Wen)

west, western, the west, western Europe

western (cowboy film)

West Bank

West Bank barrier

Should always be called a barrier when referred to in its totality, as it is in places a steel and barbed-wire fence and in others an eight-metre-high concrete wall; if referring to a particular section of it then calling it a fence or a wall may be appropriate. It can also be described as a separation barrier/fence/wall or security barrier/fence/wall, according to the nature of the article

west coast mainline

West Country

West Lothian question

Westminster Abbey

West Nile virus

Weyerhaeuser US pulp and paper company

Web style

When it comes down to it, the way Guardian Unlimited "does style" on stories is, essentially, no different to how it is done on the Guardian newspapers and magazines. Website journalists follow the online style guide in the same proudly pedantic fashion as our print counterparts. Equally, if we lapse or stray, we can rest assured that a fellow GU journalist will highlight our errors and the inevitable debates ensue over such seemingly trivial questions as when to hyphenate cash for honours (only when used as an adjective), and whether quote marks should be used around the term friendly fire (they should not).

This bread-and-butter task of subediting articles, however, is where the similarity tends to end. When it comes to doing most other webby things – writing blogs, or scripts for podcasts, or even headlines for online stories – the nature of the game changes. What game? That of attracting readers ... or users, or community members, as people who turn to the internet for their news are variously called.

And just as the overall style or feel of the writing changes between, say, the main Guardian paper and G2, so it does between the different sites on the GU network. As is to be expected of a serious news site, GU news articles conform most strictly to the style rules. By contrast, live coverage of sports matches is one of the website's most popular features, and this is largely due to its down-the-pub conversational style. Take the following example by Rob Smyth's over-by-over coverage of the second Ashes Test in 2005:

"ENGLAND HAVE WON BY 2 RUNS! THEY'VE WON! GET IN! An absolute brute of a lifter from Harmison, Kasprowicz gloved it from somewhere under his nose, and Jones – Geraint Butterfingers Flippin' Jones – took a cracking low catch to his left. A remarkable end to one of the all-time great Test matches, and some top-class stuff from the Aussies: the whole team are on the pitch shaking hands generously. Brett Lee finishes on 43 not out – a wonderful innings – and the pulse rate of Messrs Smyth and Ingle are returning to something resembling normalcy. Unbelievable stuff, and I have an appointment with the loo. Cheers for all your emails, it's been an absolute pleasure."

Similarly, when it comes to writing the scripts for podcasts, the GU audio editor, Tim Maby, says the aim is for the shows to come across as an informal discussion, ie the opposite of BBC English formality. "You are trying to spur the imagination as much as convey information," he says. "In writing for audio, aural poetry is what is possible."

As such, grammar can be more flexible and rules broken. For example, beginning sentences with conjunctions such as "and" or "but" is permissible. Equally, while keeping sentences short might help with directness, varying their length and rhythm "brings an element of fun to the job".

But again, when it comes to the actual news, things are taken slightly more seriously. Jon Dennis, the editor of GU's daily news podcast, says: "Possibly ludicrously, I try to apply our style rules where applicable, but all you can really do is strive for clarity and accuracy, adhering to good English but while sounding like a real human being."

The informal tone of the podcasts is aimed at drawing the listener in, making her feel part of the discussion. This is taken a step further on the more than 20 blogs that run on the GU network. Here, the aim is to get the reader to participate in the discussion by way of posting comments on the individual blog posts. Again, this often results in conversational writing – the author referring directly to himself in the blog post, and talking directly to the reader to elicit reaction or feedback. Take this example from Sean Ingle's post, "How do you solve a problem like kohlrabi?", on the food blog, Word of Mouth:

"When the first kohlrabi of the season arrived unannounced in our organic vegetable box last week, my wife gawped at its spacehopper belly and leafy Mr Tickle arms, before asking: what exactly is this? I suspect her reaction is not uncommon. After all, you rarely find kohlrabi in British supermarkets. Or restaurants. Or cookery books. It's big in Germany, apparently, but then so is David Hasselhoff ... So what should you do with it? ... I need help. And with the number of vegetable box schemes shooting up by the month, I'm guessing I'm not alone ... "

Putting aside the content of the website, the general nature of the internet also lends itself to different production methods for the site. Much as we would like it to be so, a significant number of people who visit GU do not come to us through our home page (www.guardian.co.uk). Instead, they come via search engines or links on other websites. This plays a big part in how subeditors headline a story. Keywords are essential if GU stories are to be found among the millions of pages being produced on the world wide web. So, for example, the headline "Attorney general responds to Bandar, £1bn and

> 'You are trying to spur the imagination as much as convey information. In writing for audio, aural poetry is what is possible'

BAE", may not be anything remarkable, but it includes all the essential words that a person might type into a search engine to find out the latest update on this particular story.

While writing headlines in this way – which in marketing-speak is part of "search engine optimisation" – causes considerable heartache for the more creative subeditor, it conversely poses a new challenge. It can be a tricky business getting enough keywords in a headline that must, again, by the very nature of website journalism, also be short, simple and active.

All the major news websites now operate in real time as users increasingly want their news now, not tomorrow. Headlines must reflect this immediacy, so the active headline "Judge jails Paris Hilton" is favoured over "Paris Hilton sent to jail" as it tells the reader this is happening now, live, click on this headline to find out more.

Equally, internet users tend to skim-read pages with lots of links on them. If we want to catch their eye, and their mouse finger, a short, snappy headline ("Bush agrees emission cuts") is more likely to tempt them to click on the story than a more descriptive but longer one ("Bush agrees to CO2 cut, with strings attached"), which works well in the newspaper, where the reader is more inclined to linger over a page and so pick up on the subtleties of a headline.

This immediacy on the internet makes for a fast-paced work environment where there are really no deadlines other than "now". Meeting this demand, however, can have its price in terms of accuracy. Copy on the website does not and is unlikely ever to undergo as much checking as it does on the paper before being published. If it did, we would lose readers to other, faster news sites. This pace, however, means there is more room for error, and this may not get picked up until the story is "live", ie published on the website for all to see. The one advantage the website has over the paper in this area is that mistakes can be quickly corrected in the actual story post-publication. But errors on the website, as in the paper, have the potential to damage the Guardian's standing as a quality news source, meaning the highest possible standards of pre-publication subediting are essential.

Just as other websites link to Guardian website content, so GU links to other sites. These appear in a variety of places on the website, eg the Environment site on GU has a page called "What can I do?" that lists links to "green" websites such as renewable energy and ethical finance providers, charities and lobby groups. Links are also put in the body of articles and blogs, or in what we call the trailblock at the bottom of articles – a list of links to useful GU pages or other websites.

Keywords are essential if GU stories are to be found among the millions of pages being produced on the world wide web

Adding the links to the body of an article requires some thought. For example, in an article about a Ministry of Defence report on recruit training it is of no use to the reader to provide a link to the MoD home page, as this then requires them to search that site for the relevant report. Rather, the article should link directly to the report. In terms of how that link is provided, it is best to put it in an active part of an existing sentence, eg "In a report released today by the MoD ... ", or alternatively, "The MoD report said ... ". Terms such as "click here" are to be avoided. Also, it is important to provide only strictly relevant links if articles are not to become too link-heavy. In the MoD example, a link to the report is good, but while a link to a Wikipedia page about the British army may be interesting, it is not strictly relevant to the subject of the article.

Since it began in 1999, Guardian Unlimited has been constantly evolving to keep pace not only with internet technology but also with the demands of web users and, of course, the competition. Podcasts, blogs, online debates, audio slideshows, live event coverage, videos ... each has added a new dimension to the increasingly large network of sites that falls under the name Guardian Unlimited. But GU is still, ultimately, a product of the Guardian, and its style, in the broadest possible sense, is and will continue to be a reflection of that.

guardian style

what is a phrase that, while occasionally helpful to add emphasis, has become overused to the point of tedium; examples from the paper include:

"Beckham repaid the committed public support with what was a man-of-the-match performance ... "

"Principal among Schofield's 19 recommendations in what is a wide-ranging report ... "

What is clear is that these would be improved by what would be the simple step of removing the offending phrase

wheelchair say (if relevant) that someone uses a wheelchair, not that they are "in a wheelchair" or "wheelchair-bound" – stigmatising and offensive, as well as inaccurate

Memo to your
contributors re the
use of the word
"whence". The
word means
"where from". Too
many write "from
whence". My old
English teacher
must be spinning!
Phil Jones, Wirral

whence means where from, so don't write "from whence"

whereabouts singular: her whereabouts is not known

which or **that**? *see that or which?*

Which? the magazine, and the organisation that publishes it

while not whilst

whisky plural whiskies; but Irish and US **whiskey**

whistleblower

white lc in racial context

white paper

white van man

Whitsuntide not Whitsun

whiz, whiz-kid

318

who or whom?

From a Guardian report: "The US kept up the pressure by naming nine Yugoslav military leaders operating in Kosovo whom it said were committing war crimes." The "whom" should have been "who". That one was caught by the subeditor, but it is a common mistake.

If in doubt, ask yourself how the clause beginning who/whom would read in the form of a sentence giving he, him, she, her, they or them instead: if the who/whom person turns into he/she/they, then "who" is right; if it becomes him/her/them, then it should be "whom".

In the story above, "they" were allegedly committing the crimes, so it should be "who".

In this example: "Brown was criticised for attacking Cameron, whom he despised" – "whom" is correct because he despised "him".

But in "Brown attacked Cameron, who he thought was wrong" – "who" is correct, because it is "he" not "him" who is considered wrong.

Use of "whom" has all but disappeared from spoken English, and seems to be going the same way in most forms of written English too. If you are not sure, it is much better to use "who" when "whom" would traditionally have been required than to use "whom" incorrectly for "who", which will make you look not just wrong but wrong and pompous

whodunit

wicketkeeper

Widdecombe, Ann Tory cabinet minister who, briefly, became a Guardian agony aunt

wide awake

Wiesel, Elie Holocaust survivor and author, awarded the Nobel peace prize in 1986

Wi-Fi TM; the generic term is **wireless computer network**

Ww

Wii
– witchcraft

guardian style

Wii Nintendo games machine

Willans, Geoffrey (not Williams or Willians, as have appeared in the paper) author of the Molesworth books, illustrated by Ronald Searle, as any fule kno

Wimpey houses; **Wimpy** burgers

windbag, windfall, windpipe, windscreen

Windermere not Lake Windermere; note that Windermere is also the name of the town

wines normally lc, whether taking their name from a region (eg beaujolais, bordeaux, burgundy, chablis, champagne) or a grape variety (eg cabernet sauvignon, chardonnay, merlot, muscadet).
The regions themselves are capped up: so one might drink a burgundy from Burgundy, or a muscadet from the Loire valley; as are wines of individual chateaux, eg I enjoyed a glass of Cos d'Estournel 1970

wing commander in leading articles, abbreviate on second mention to Wing Co; Wing Commander Barry Johnson, subsequently Wing Co Johnson; otherwise just Johnson

Winnie-the-Pooh in the original AA Milne books, although the "bear of little brain" has lost the hyphens in his Disney incarnation

winter

winter of discontent

wipeout noun; **wipe out** verb

wishlist

witchcraft but **witch-doctor, witch-hunt**

withhold

witness not eyewitness, except for the Eyewitness picture spread in the Guardian

wits' end

woeful

woman, women are nouns, not adjectives, so say female president, female MPs, etc rather than "woman president", "women MPs"

womenswear but the magazine is **Women's Wear Daily**

Woolworths

Worcestershire sauce not Worcester

working class noun; **working-class** adjective

working tax credit replaced the working families tax credit

World Bank

world championship

World Cup football, cricket or rugby

World Food Programme may be abbreviated to WFP after first mention

> Can I ask you to consider whether you need to use the word "principality" – or, even worse, "Principality" – in future? Since it manages to effortlessly combine monarchism and colonialism, it sticks in many a craw here.
>
> **Huw Roberts, Cardiff**

World Health Organisation WHO on second mention

world heritage site

World Series

It is a myth that this baseball event got its name from the New York World: originally known as the World's Championship Series, it had nothing to do with the newspaper.

It has become tedious every time the World Series comes round to see its name cited as an example of American arrogance, so please don't do it

World Trade Centre, Ground Zero but the **twin towers**

worldwide often redundant, eg "it has automotive plants in 30 countries worldwide" (as opposed to galaxy-wide?)

world wide web

would-be

wrack seaweed; **racked** with guilt and shame, not wracked; **rack and ruin**

wrinklies patronising, unfunny way to refer to elderly people; do not use

wuss

WWE World Wrestling Entertainment, formerly the World Wrestling Federation

WWF formerly the World Wide Fund for Nature (or, in the US, World Wildlife Fund)

X x

"Editors are craftsmen, ghosts, psychiatrists,
bullies, sparring partners, experts, enablers,
ignoramuses, translators, writers, goalies,
friends, foremen, wimps, ditch diggers,
mind readers, coaches, bomb throwers,
muses and spittoons — sometimes all while
working on the same piece."

Gary Kamiya, Salon.com

Xbox

xenophobe, xenophobia, xenophobic

Xerox TM; say **photocopy**

Xhosa South African ethnic group and language

Xi'an city in China where the Terracotta Warriors are located

Xmas avoid; use Christmas unless writing a headline, up against a deadline, and desperate

x-ray

I am becoming increasingly concerned at the number of Guardian headlines which report someone's "fury" at an event rather than the event itself. This seems to be an old tabloid trick (when "anger at ... " became just too dull) and leads me to suspect that you have recently employed an ex-Sun subeditor to work weekends! Predicting the emotional state of someone you don't know seems a little presumptuous, to say the least.

Gary Austin, Swanage, Dorset

Yy

"Anyone not acquainted with
journalists could be forgiven for
assuming that they must talk
something like this: 'I last night
went to bed early because I this
morning had to catch an early
flight.'"

Bill Bryson

y or ie?

As a general rule: -y is an English suffix, whose function is to create an adjective (usually from a noun, eg creamy); -ie was originally a Scottish suffix, whose function is to add the meaning of "diminutive" (usually from a noun, eg beastie).

So in most cases, where there is dispute over whether a noun takes a -y or -ie ending, the correct answer is -ie: she's a girly girl, but she's no helpless girlie. Think also scrunchie, beanie, nightie, meanie ... There are exceptions (a hippy, an indie band), but where specific examples are not given, use -ie for nouns and -y for adjectives

Yahoo (the company) no exclamation mark

Yangtze river not Yangtse

Yar'Adua, Umaru succeeded Olusegun Obasanjo as president of Nigeria in 2007

year say 2007, not "the year 2007"; for a span of years use hyphen, thus: 2007-08, not 2007/8

year 1, year 10 etc (schools)

yearbook

Yekaterinburg

Yellow Pages TM

Yemen not the Yemen

yes campaign, no campaign not Yes or "yes" campaign

yesterday take care where you place the time element in a story: do not automatically place it at the start ("Gordon Brown last night insisted ... "). Constructions such as "the two sides were today to consider", as we have been known to say, sound ugly and artificial. As with headlines, try reading out loud to find the most natural arrangement

yoghurt

York Minster

Yorkshire use **North Yorkshire, South Yorkshire, West Yorkshire** but **east Yorkshire**

Yorkshire dales but **North York Moors** national park

yorkshire pudding, yorkshire terrier

Yorkshire Ripper

Young, Lady Lady Young of Old Scone, chief executive of the Environment Agency; Lady Young of Hornsey, artist and teacher. Lady Young of Farnworth, a former Tory leader of the Lords and staunch defender of section 28, died in 2002

young turks

Young Visiters, The (not Visitors) novel by the Victorian child author Daisy Ashford, filmed by the BBC in 2003

yours no apostrophe

YouTube

yo-yo

Yo-Yo Ma cellist

yuan Chinese currency; we don't call it renminbi

Yu-Gi-Oh!

yuletide

Reference "In praise of the subeditor" (Guardian, November 13 2006) – I'm sorry, but you'll need to make a better case for subeditors than this: "Newspapers have found it difficulty to recruit subeditors over the last few years." As Private Eye used to have it: Shome mishtake here shurely!

Jonathan Kemp,
Eastleigh, Hampshire

Zz

"I am about to – or I am going to – die;
either expression is used."

**Last words of the 17th-century
French Jesuit grammarian
Dominique Bouhours**

Zanu-PF Zimbabwe's ruling party; the opposition, led by Morgan Tsvangirai, is the Movement for Democratic Change (MDC)

Zapatero, José Luis Rodríguez Spanish politician, elected prime minister in 2004; Zapatero on second mention

-ze endings

Use -se, even if this upsets your (American) spellchecker, eg emphasise, realise; but **capsize**

zeitgeist

Zellweger, Renée

Zephaniah, Benjamin

zero plural **zeros**

Zeta-Jones, Catherine

zeugma an example: "The queen takes counsel and tea" (Alexander Pope)

zhoosh an example of gay slang (*see Polari*), used in the fashion industry and on US television shows such as Will and Grace and Queer Eye for the Straight Guy, it has various shades of meaning: (noun) clothing, ornamentation; (verb) zhoosh your hair, zhoosh yourself up; **zhooshy** (adjective) showy

Zhu Rongji Chinese premier (prime minister) from 1998 to 2003, when he was succeeded by Wen Jiabao

zigzag no hyphen

Zimmer TM; if it's not a Zimmer frame, call it a **walking frame**

Zionist refers to someone who believes in the right for a Jewish national home to exist within historic Palestine; someone who wants the borders of that entity to be expanded is not an "ultra-Zionist" but might be described as a hardliner, hawk or rightwinger

zloty Polish unit of currency

zoos lc: London zoo, San Diego zoo, etc

A preschooler's tacit knowledge of grammar is more sophisticated than the thickest style manual.

Steven Pinker

References

www.guardian.co.uk/styleguide

Amis, Kingsley: The King's English: A Guide to Modern Usage (HarperCollins, 1997)

Baker, Paul: Fantabulosa, A Dictionary of Polari and Gay Slang (Continuum, 2002)

Bauer, Laurie and Trudgill, Peter (eds): Language Myths (Penguin, 1998)

Bierce, Ambrose: The Devil's Dictionary (Neal Publishing Company, 1911; reprinted by Dover Publications, 1993)

Bryson, Bill: Mother Tongue (Penguin, 1991)

Bryson, Bill: Troublesome Words (Viking, 3rd edition, 2001)

Burchfield, RW: The Spoken Word (BBC Books, 1981)

Burchfield, RW: The New Fowler's Modern English Usage (Oxford University Press, revised 3rd edition, 1998)

Collins English Dictionary (HarperCollins, 8th edition, 2006)

Crystal, David: The Cambridge Encyclopedia of English (Cambridge University Press, 1995)

Crystal, David: Who Cares About English Usage? (Penguin, 2nd edition, 2000)

Crystal, David: Fight for English: How Language Pundits Ate, Shot and Left (OUP, 2006)

Crystal, David: Language and the Internet (Cambridge University Press, revised 2nd edition, 2006)

The Economist Style Guide (Profile Books, 2005)

Hicks, Wynford: Writing for Journalists (Routledge, 2nd edition, 1998)

Hicks, Wynford and Holmes, Tim: Subediting for Journalists (Routledge, 2002)

Huddleston, Rodney: Introduction to the Grammar of English (Cambridge University Press, 1984)

Inman, Colin: The Financial Times Style Guide (Pitman, 1994)

Martin, Paul R: The Wall Street Journal Guide to Business Style and Usage (Free Press, 2002)

Miller, Casey and Swift, Kate: The Handbook of Non-Sexist Writing for Writers, Editors and Speakers (The Women's Press, 1980)

Oxford English Dictionary online: http://dictionary.oed.com

Palmer, FR: The English Verb (Longman, 2nd edition, 1988)

Poole, Steven: Unspeak (Little, Brown, 2006)

Quirk, R; Greenbaum, S; Leech, G; Svartvik, J: A Comprehensive Grammar of the English Language (Longman, 1985)

Pinker, Steven: The Language Instinct (Penguin, 1994)

Pinker, Steven: Words and Rules (Phoenix, 1999)

Siegal, Alan M and Connolly, William G: The New York Times Manual of Style and Usage (Times Books, 1999)

Trask, RL: Mind the Gaffe (Penguin, 2001)

Appendix 1

The Guardian's editorial code
(incorporating the Press Complaints Commission code of practice)

(updated April 2007)

Summary

"A newspaper's primary office is the gathering of news. At the peril of its soul it must see that the supply is not tainted."

The most important currency of the Guardian is trust. This is as true today as when CP Scott marked the centenary of the founding of the newspaper with his famous essay on journalism in 1921.

The purpose of this code is, above all, to protect and foster the bond of trust between the Guardian (in print and online) and its readers, and therefore to protect the integrity of the paper and of the editorial content it carries.

As a set of guidelines this will not form part of a journalist's contract of employment, nor will it form part, for either editorial management or journalists, of disciplinary, promotional or recruitment procedures. However, by observing the code, journalists working for the Guardian will be protecting not only the paper but also the independence, standing and reputation of themselves and their colleagues. It is important that freelancers working for the Guardian also abide by these guidelines while on assignment for the paper.

Press Complaints Commission code of practice

The Guardian – in common with most other papers in Britain – considers the PCC's code of practice to be a sound statement of ethical behaviour for journalists. It is written into our terms of employment that staff should adhere to the code of practice. It is published below so that all editorial staff can familiarise themselves with it – and comments in this document that relate to the PCC code are marked with an asterisk.

1 Professional practice

Anonymous quotations

We recognise that people will often speak more honestly if they are allowed to speak anonymously. The use of non-attributed quotes can therefore often assist the reader towards a truer understanding of a subject than if a journalist confined him/herself to quoting bland on-the-record quotes. But if used lazily or indiscriminately anonymous quotes become a menace.

We should be honest about our sources, even if we can't name them.

The New York Times policy on pejorative quotes is worth bearing in mind: "The vivid language of direct quotation confers an unfair advantage on a speaker or writer who hides behind the newspaper, and turns of phrase are valueless to a reader who cannot assess the source."

There may be exceptional circumstances when anonymous pejorative quotes may be used, but they will be rare – and only after consultation with the senior editor of the day. In the absence of specific approval we should paraphrase anonymous pejorative quotes.

Children *

Special care should be taken when dealing with children (under the age of 16). Heads of departments must be informed when children have been photographed or interviewed without parental consent.

(See PCC code, section 6)

Copy approval

The general rule is that no one should be given the right to copy approval. In certain circumstances we may allow people to see copy or quotes but we are not required to alter copy. We should avoid offering copy approval as a method of securing interviews or cooperation.

Direct quotations

Should not be changed to alter their context or meaning.

Errors

It is the policy of the Guardian to correct significant errors as soon as possible. Journalists have a duty to cooperate frankly and openly with the readers' editor and to report errors to her. All complaints should be brought to the attention of a department head, the managing editor or the readers' editor. All journalists should read both the daily and weekly column.

Fairness

"The voice of opponents no less than of friends has a right to be heard ...
It is well be to be frank; it is even better to be fair." (CP Scott, 1921)
The more serious the criticism or allegations we are reporting, the greater the obligation to allow the subject the opportunity to respond.

Grief *

People should be treated with sensitivity during periods of grief and trauma.
(See PCC code, section 5)

Language

Respect for the reader demands that we should not casually use words that are likely to offend. Use swearwords only when absolutely necessary to the facts of a piece, or to portray a character in an article; there is almost never a case in which we need to use a swearword outside direct quotes. The stronger the swearword, the harder we ought to think about using it. Avoid using in headlines, pullquotes and standfirsts and never use asterisks, which are just a cop-out.

Legal

Our libel and contempt laws are complex, and constantly developing. The consequences of losing actions can be expensive and damaging for our reputation. Staff should a) familiarise themselves with the current state of the law and seek training if they feel unconfident about aspects of it; b) consult our in-house legal department or night lawyers about specific concerns on stories; c) read the regular legal bulletins about active cases and injunctions emailed by the legal department.

Payment

In general, the Guardian does not pay for stories, except from bona fide freelance sources. The editor or his deputies must approve rare exceptions.

PCC and libel judgments

Judgments by the PCC and the outcome of defamation actions relating to the Guardian should be reported promptly.

Photographs

Digitally enhanced or altered images, montages and illustrations should be clearly labeled as such.

Plagiarism

Staff must not reproduce other people's material without attribution. The source of published material obtained from another organisation should be acknowledged, including quotes taken from other newspaper articles. Bylines should be carried only on material that is substantially the work of the bylined journalist. If an article contains a significant amount of agency copy then the agency should be credited.

Privacy

In keeping with both the PCC code and the Human Rights Act we believe in respecting people's privacy. We should avoid intrusions into people's privacy unless there is a clear public interest in doing so. Caution should be exercised about reporting and publishing identifying details, such as street names and numbers, that may enable others to intrude on the

privacy or safety of people who have become the subject of
media coverage.

Race

In general, we do not publish someone's race or ethnic
background or religion unless that information is pertinent to
the story. We do not report the race of criminal suspects unless
their ethnic background is part of a description that seeks to
identify them or is an important part of the story (for example,
if the crime was a hate crime).

Sources

Sources promised confidentiality must be protected at all costs.
However, where possible, the sources of information should be
identified as specifically as possible.

Subterfuge

Journalists should generally identify themselves as Guardian
employees when working on a story. There may be instances
involving stories of exceptional public interest where this
does not apply, but this needs the approval of a head of
department.

Suicide

Journalists are asked to exercise particular care in reporting
suicide or issues involving suicide, bearing in mind the risk of
encouraging others. This should be borne in mind both in
presentation, including the use of pictures, and in describing the
method of suicide. Any substances should be referred to in
general rather than specific terms if possible. When appropriate
a helpline number should be given (eg Samaritans 08457 909090).
The feelings of relatives should also be carefully considered.

2 Personal behaviour and conflicts of interest

The Guardian values its reputation for independence and
integrity. Journalists clearly have lives, interests, hobbies,
convictions and beliefs outside their work on the paper. Nothing

in the following guidelines is intended to restrict any of that. It is intended to ensure that outside interests do not come into conflict with the life of the paper in a way that either compromises the Guardian's editorial integrity or falls short of the sort of transparency that our readers would expect. The code is intended to apply to all active outside interests which, should they remain undeclared and become known, would cause a fair-minded reader to question the value of a contribution to the paper by the journalist involved.

These are guidelines rather than one-size-fits-all rules. If you are employed as a columnist – with your views openly on display – you may have more latitude than a staff reporter, who would be expected to bring qualities of objectivity to their work. (The Washington Post's code has some sound advice: "Reporters should make every effort to remain in the audience, to stay off the stage, to report the news, not to make the news.") If in doubt, consult a head of department, the managing or deputy editors, or the editor himself.

Commercial products
No Guardian journalist or freelance primarily associated with the Guardian should endorse commercial products unless with the express permission of their head of department or managing editor.

Confidentiality
Desk editors with access to personal information relating to other members of staff are required to treat such information as confidential, and not disclose it to anyone except in the course of discharging formal responsibilities.

Conflicts of interest
Guardian staff journalists should be sensitive to the possibility that activities outside work (including holding office or being otherwise actively involved in organisations, companies or political parties) could be perceived as having a bearing on – or as coming into conflict with – the integrity of our journalism. Staff should be transparent about any outside personal, philosophical or financial interests that might conflict with their

professional performance of duties at the Guardian, or could be perceived to do so.

Declarations of interest

1 It is always necessary to declare an interest when the journalist is writing about something with which he or she has a significant connection. This applies to both staff journalists and freelances writing for the Guardian. The declaration should be to a head of department or editor during preparation. Full transparency may mean that the declaration should appear in the paper or website as well.

2 A connection does not have to be a formal one before it is necessary to declare it. Acting in an advisory capacity in the preparation of a report for an organisation, for example, would require a declaration every time the journalist wrote an article referring to it.

3 Some connections are obvious and represent the reason why the writer has been asked to contribute to the paper. These should always be stated at the end of the writer's contribution even if he or she contributes regularly, so long as the writer is writing about his or her area of interest.

4 Generally speaking a journalist should not write about or quote a relative or partner in a piece, even if the relative or partner is an expert in the field in question. If, for any reason, an exception is made to this rule, the connection should be made clear.

5 Commissioning editors should ensure that freelances asked to write for the Guardian are aware of these rules and make any necessary declaration.

Declarations of corporate interest

The Guardian is part of a wider group of media companies. We should be careful to acknowledge that relationship in stories. Anyone writing a story concerning Guardian-related businesses should seek comments and/or confirmation in the normal way. Staff should familiarise themselves with the companies and interests we have.

Financial reporting

For many years the Guardian's business desk has maintained a register of personal shares. All staff are expected to list all shares that they own, any transactions in those shares and any other investments that they believe ought to be properly disclosed because of a potential conflict of interest. While it is acceptable for financial members to own shares, it is not acceptable for them to be market traders on a regular basis. It is most important that the register is kept and that all information is up to date. The attention of Guardian journalists is also drawn to section 13 of the PCC code of practice (below) and to the PCC's best-practice guidelines on financial journalism, which can also be found in the "code advice" section of the PCC website.

The code: prohibits the use of financial information for the profit of journalists or their associates; imposes restrictions on journalists writing about shares in which they or their close families have a significant interest without internal disclosure; stops journalists dealing in shares about which they have written recently or intend to write in the near future; requires that financial journalists take care not to publish inaccurate material and to distinguish between comment, conjecture and fact. This is particularly important for any journalists making investment recommendations to readers about whether to buy, sell or hold shares.

Freebies

1 Staff should not use their position to obtain private benefit for themselves or others.
2 The Guardian and its staff will not allow any payment, gift or other advantage to undermine accuracy, fairness or independence. Any attempts to induce favourable editorial treatment through the offer of gifts or favours should be reported to the editor. Where relevant the Guardian will disclose these payments, gifts or other advantages.
3 We should make it clear when an airline, hotel or other interest has borne the cost of transporting or accommodating a journalist. Acceptance of any such offer is conditional on

the Guardian being free to assign and report or not report any resulting story as it sees fit.

4 Except in some areas of travel writing it should never need to be the case that the journalist's partner, family or friends are included in any free arrangement. When a partner, family member or friend accompanies the journalist on a trip, the additional costs should generally be paid for by the journalist or person accompanying the journalist.

5 Staff should not be influenced by commercial considerations – including the interests of advertisers – in the preparation of material for the paper.

6 Gifts other than those of an insignificant value (say, less than £25) should be politely returned or may be entered for the annual raffle of such items for charity, the "sleaze raffle".

Freelance work

As a general rule avoid freelance writing for house magazines of particular businesses or causes if the contribution could be interpreted as an endorsement of the concern. If in doubt consult your head or department.

Guardian connections

Staff members should not use their positions at the Guardian to seek any benefit or advantage in personal business, financial or commercial transactions not afforded to the public generally. Staff should not use Guardian stationery in connection with non-Guardian matters or cite a connection with the paper to resolve consumer grievances, get quicker service or seek discount or deals.

Outside engagements or duties

The Guardian accepts the journalist's right to a private life and the right to take part in civic society. However, staff should inform their immediate editor if, in their capacity as an employee of the Guardian, they intend to:

1 Give evidence to any court.

2 Chair public forums or seminars arranged by professional conference organisers or commercial organisations.

3   Undertake any outside employment likely to conflict with their professional duties at the Guardian.
4   Chair public or political forums or appear on platforms.
5   Make representations or give evidence to any official body in connection with material that has been published in the Guardian.

Relationships

Staff members should not write about, photograph or make news judgments about any individual related by blood or marriage or with whom the staff member has a close personal, financial or romantic relationship. A staff member who is placed in a circumstance in which the potential for this kind of conflict exists should advise his or her department head.

Press Complaints Commission code of practice

The Press Complaints Commission is charged with enforcing the following code of practice, which was framed by the newspaper and periodical industry and was ratified by the PCC on August 7 2006. Clauses marked * are covered by exceptions related to the public interest.

The code

All members of the press have a duty to maintain the highest professional standards. This code sets the benchmark for those ethical standards, protecting both the rights of the individual and the public's right to know. It is the cornerstone of the system of self-regulation to which the industry has made a binding commitment.

It is essential that an agreed code be honoured not only to the letter but in the full spirit. It should not be interpreted so narrowly as to compromise its commitment to respect the rights of the individual, nor so broadly that it constitutes an unnecessary interference with freedom of expression or prevents publication in the public interest.

It is the responsibility of editors and publishers to implement the code and they should take care to ensure it is observed rigorously by all editorial staff and external contributors, including non-journalists, in printed and online versions of publications. Editors should co-operate swiftly with the PCC in the resolution of complaints. Any publication judged to have breached the code must print the adjudication in full and with due prominence, including headline reference to the PCC.

1 Accuracy

i The press must take care not to publish inaccurate, misleading or distorted information, including pictures.

ii A significant inaccuracy, misleading statement or distortion once recognised must be corrected, promptly and with due prominence, and – where appropriate – an apology published.

iii The press, whilst free to be partisan, must distinguish clearly between comment, conjecture and fact.

iv A publication must report fairly and accurately the outcome of an action for defamation to which it has been a party, unless an agreed settlement states otherwise, or an agreed statement is published.

2 Opportunity to reply

A fair opportunity for reply to inaccuracies must be given when reasonably called for.

3 * Privacy

i Everyone is entitled to respect for his or her private and family life, home, health and correspondence, including digital communications. Editors will be expected to justify intrusions into any individual's private life without consent.

ii It is unacceptable to photograph individuals in private places without their consent.

Note: Private places are public or private property where there is a reasonable expectation of privacy.

4 * Harassment

i Journalists must not engage in intimidation, harassment or persistent pursuit.

ii They must not persist in questioning, telephoning, pursuing or photographing individuals once asked to desist; nor remain on their property when asked to leave and must not follow them.

iii Editors must ensure these principles are observed by those working for them and take care not to use non-compliant material from other sources.

5 Intrusion into grief or shock

i In cases involving personal grief or shock, enquiries and approaches must be made with sympathy and discretion and publication handled sensitively. This should not restrict the right to report legal proceedings, such as inquests.

* ii When reporting suicide, care should be taken to avoid excessive detail about the method used.

6 * Children

i Young people should be free to complete their time at school without unnecessary intrusion.

ii A child under 16 must not be interviewed or photographed on issues involving their own or another child's welfare unless a custodial parent or similarly responsible adult consents.

iii Pupils must not be approached or photographed at school without the permission of the school authorities.

iv Minors must not be paid for material involving children's welfare, nor parents or guardians for material about their children or wards, unless it is clearly in the child's interest.

v Editors must not use the fame, notoriety or position of a parent or guardian as sole justification for publishing details of a child's private life.

7 * Children in sex cases

1 The press must not, even if legally free to do so, identify children under 16 who are victims or witnesses in cases involving sex offences.

2 In any press report of a case involving a sexual offence against a child:

   i. the child must not be identified;

   ii. the adult may be identified:

   iii. the word "incest" must not be used where a child victim might be identified:

   iv. care must be taken that nothing in the report implies the relationship between the accused and the child.

8 * Hospitals

i Journalists must identify themselves and obtain permission from a responsible executive before entering non-public areas of hospitals or similar institutions to pursue enquiries.

ii The restrictions on intruding into privacy are particularly relevant to enquiries about individuals in hospitals or similar institutions.

9 * Reporting of crime

i Relatives or friends of persons convicted or accused of crime should not generally be identified without their consent, unless they are genuinely relevant to the story.

ii Particular regard should be paid to the potentially vulnerable position of children who witness, or are victims of, crime. This should not restrict the right to report legal proceedings.

10 * Clandestine devices and subterfuge

i The press must not seek to obtain or publish material acquired by using hidden cameras or clandestine listening devices; or by intercepting private or mobile telephone calls, messages or emails; or by the unauthorised removal of documents or photographs.

ii Engaging in misrepresentation or subterfuge, can generally be justified only in the public interest and then only when the material cannot be obtained by other means.

11 Victims of sexual assault

The press must not identify victims of sexual assault or publish material likely to contribute to such identification unless there is adequate justification and they are legally free to do so.

12 Discrimination

i The press must avoid prejudicial or pejorative reference to an individual's race, colour, religion, gender, sexual orientation or to any physical or mental illness or disability.

ii Details of an individual's race, colour, religion, sexual orientation, physical or mental illness or disability must be avoided unless genuinely relevant to the story.

13 Financial journalism

i Even where the law does not prohibit it, journalists must not use for their own profit financial information they receive in advance of its general publication, nor should they pass such information to others.

ii They must not write about shares or securities in whose performance they know that they or their close families have a significant financial interest without disclosing the interest to the editor or financial editor.

iii They must not buy or sell, either directly or through
nominees or agents, shares or securities about which they
have written recently or about which they intend to write in
the near future.

14 Confidential sources

Journalists have a moral obligation to protect confidential
sources of information.

15 Witness payments in criminal trials

i No payment or offer of payment to a witness – or any
person who may reasonably be expected to be called as a
witness – should be made in any case once proceedings are
active as defined by the Contempt of Court Act 1981.

This prohibition lasts until the suspect has been freed
unconditionally by police without charge or bail or the
proceedings are otherwise discontinued; or has entered a
guilty plea to the court; or, in the event of a not guilty
plea, the court has announced its verdict.

* ii Where proceedings are not yet active but are likely and
foreseeable, editors must not make or offer payment to any
person who may reasonably be expected to be called as a
witness, unless the information concerned ought
demonstrably to be published in the public interest and
there is an over-riding need to make or promise payment
for this to be done; and all reasonable steps have been taken
to ensure no financial dealings influence the evidence those
witnesses give. In no circumstances should such payment
be conditional on the outcome of a trial.

* iii Any payment or offer of payment made to a person later
cited to give evidence in proceedings must be disclosed to
the prosecution and defence. The witness must be advised
of this requirement.

16 * Payment to criminals

i Payment or offers of payment for stories, pictures or
information, which seek to exploit a particular crime or to
glorify or glamorise crime in general, must not be made

directly or via agents to convicted or confessed criminals or to their associates – who may include family, friends and colleagues.

ii Editors invoking the public interest to justify payment or offers would need to demonstrate that there was good reason to believe the public interest would be served. If, despite payment, no public interest emerged, then the material should not be published.

The public interest

There may be exceptions to the clauses marked * where they can be demonstrated to be in the public interest.

1 The public interest includes, but is not confined to:
   i   Detecting or exposing crime or serious impropriety;
   ii Protecting public health and safety;
   iii Preventing the public from being misled by an action or statement of an individual or organisation.

2 There is a public interest in freedom of expression itself.

3 Whenever the public interest is invoked, the PCC will require editors to demonstrate fully how the public interest was served.

4 The PCC will consider the extent to which material is already in the public domain, or will become so.

5 In cases involving children under 16, editors must demonstrate an exceptional public interest to over-ride the normally paramount interest of the child.

Appendix 2

The editor's guidelines on the identification of sources

We should use anonymous sources sparingly. We should – except in exceptional circumstances – avoid anonymous pejorative quotes. We should avoid misrepresenting the nature and number of sources, and we should do our best to give readers some clue as to the authority with which they speak. We should never, ever, betray a source.

We all understand the reasons why. People will frequently only say interesting and important things if they can do so anonymously. Sometimes the reasons are ignoble (cowardice), sometimes noble (whistleblowing). At Westminster, in particular, what is accurate is often not on the record. So, obviously, much has to be left to the judgment of the reporter. Sometimes the sensitivity may be such that writers may even have to be economical with the truth in identifying the nature of the source. Such occasions should be rare.

Anonymous pejorative quotes may only be used after consultation with the senior editor of the day. In taking the decision whether to allow the quote the editor might consider such factors as:

Is the source a respected person who is well-placed to pass judgment on the subject in question?

Does he/she have direct or indirect knowledge? Is it authoritative?

Insofar as one can judge, what are his or her motives in a) speaking pejoratively of someone, and b) demanding anonymity?

Can a public interest case be made for including the information in direct quotes?

In the absence of specific approval we should paraphrase anonymous pejorative quotes.

In all this, Guardian journalists simply have to bear in mind the innocent reader, and the cumulative effect of ploughing through a paper in which a significant degree of information is passed on without any means of knowing how to evaluate it. We're effectively asking readers to take a lot on trust. And the one thing we know from all surveys is that readers are increasingly sceptical about placing their trust in newspapers (though, thankfully, Guardian readers place a very great degree of trust in the Guardian).

It is – obviously – preferable if you can persuade a source to go on the record. Where this is out of the question think of the poor reader and try and give him/her some help. "One source said last night" is, in most circumstances, so vague as to be meaningless. The reader cannot evaluate the worth of the quote, as he/she has absolutely no clue as to who the source is or whether it knows what it is talking about.

If vagueness is the only option, is it possible to explain why, or to elaborate on the understanding between source and reporter? Better still is to press your source for some form of identification. So, it is best to be a specific as possible. "One MP", or "a government colleague" is so weak as to be meaningless. "Senior minister" is an advance. "Cabinet minister with direct knowledge of the negotiations" is better still. By now the reader can genuinely evaluate the worth of the remark.

I know you know that the most vaguely sourced story can also be the most authoritative. Just remember that the reader doesn't.

There is a similar difficulty in trying to set a rule of thumb about the number of sources we need before we'll print something. It's pretty obvious that it's generally good journalistic practice to speak to as many people as possible in putting together a story. You test the information Source A gives you against the information Source B gives you. You may even be reluctant to ring Source C in case he/she knocks down the story from Sources A and B. Ring Source C.

Equally, there are instances when a person you know to be truthful tells you something from his or her own personal knowledge. If the Archbishop of Canterbury rang to tell you he was resigning tomorrow, you'd print it.

The difficulty comes where a reliable, well-placed and knowledgeable source mixes information of which he/she has personal, first-hand knowledge, with material of which he/she has less direct knowledge. He/she may, in other words, be a good, single source for some information, while other parts – from the same person – would require verification from another source.

Any reporter who has spent more than a morning in court learns the difference between hearsay evidence and direct evidence. One carries weight in court, the other doesn't. Journalism can seldom aspire to be as rigorous as legal proceedings. But we should bear in mind that fundamental distinction between types of information and types of source, if for no other reason that your story might end up in court.

A good general rule might be this: stories should wherever possible be multi-sourced. Where that is not possible, the reliance on a single source should be made clear to desk editors and the matter discussed fully. The desk editor may well ask about such matters as: why there is no other way of verifying the story; whether the single source is trusted and in a position to know what they are divulging to us; and whether the story is in the public interest. If there is a chance that additional sources could be obtained by holding off publication by a day or even a few days, then we may want to wait, unless there is an overwhelming need – not just the general desire for competitive edge – to get the story out immediately.

Finally, we should, as ever, guard against the lazy habit of using quotes from other papers when pressed at deadline – and we should always attribute the source of any such lifted quotes. Wherever possible we should strive to speak directly to relevant parties.

This is a counsel of perfection. We will sometimes, for any number of reasons, slip below these standards. That doesn't mean that we shouldn't aspire to them. There are individual departments and specialisms – City and intelligence matters – where sourcing is particularly difficult. But, over time, the more careful and watchful we are the more we will be trusted – by both readers and sources.

Appendix 3

CP Scott's 1921 essay on the centenary of the Manchester Guardian

Thursday May 5 1921

A hundred years is a long time; it is a long time even in the life of a newspaper, and to look back on it is to take in not only a vast development in the thing itself, but a great slice in the life of the nation, in the progress and adjustment of the world.

In the general development the newspaper, as an institution, has played its part, and no small part, and the particular newspaper with which I personally am concerned has also played its part, it is to be hoped, not without some usefulness. I have had my share in it for a little more than fifty years; I have been its responsible editor for only a few months short of its last half-century; I remember vividly its fiftieth birthday; I now have the happiness to share in the celebration of its hundredth. I can therefore speak of it with a certain intimacy of acquaintance. I have myself been part of it and entered into its inner courts. That is perhaps a reason why, on this occasion, I should write in my own name, as in some sort a spectator, rather than in the name of the paper as a member of its working staff.

In all living things there must be a certain unity, a principle of vitality and growth. It is so with a newspaper, and the more complete and clear this unity the more vigorous and fruitful the growth. I ask myself what the paper stood for when first I knew it, what it has stood for since and stands for now.

A newspaper has two sides to it. It is a business, like any other, and has to pay in the material sense in order to live. But it is much more than a business; it is an institution; it reflects and it influences the life of a whole community; it may affect even wider destinies. It is, in its way, an instrument of government. It plays on the minds and consciences of men. It may educate, stimulate, assist, or it may do the opposite. It has, therefore, a moral as well as a material existence, and its character and influence are in the main determined by the balance of these two forces. It may make profit or power its first object, or it may conceive itself as fulfilling a higher and more exacting function.

I think I may honestly say that, from the day of its foundation, there has not been much doubt as to which way the balance tipped as far as regards the conduct of the paper whose fine tradition I inherited and which I have had the honour to serve through all my working life. Had it not been so, personally, I could not have served it. Character is a subtle affair, and has many shades and sides to it. It is not a thing to be much talked about, but rather to be felt. It is the slow deposit of past actions and ideals. It is for each man his most precious possession, and so it is for that latest growth of time the newspaper. Fundamentally it implies honesty, cleanness, courage, fairness, a sense of duty to the reader and the community. A newspaper is of necessity something of a monopoly, and its first duty is to shun the temptations of monopoly. Its primary office is the gathering of news. At the peril of its soul it must see that the supply is not tainted. Neither in what it gives, nor in what it does not give, nor in the mode of presentation must the unclouded face of truth suffer wrong. Comment is free, but facts are sacred. "Propaganda," so called, by this means is hateful. The voice of opponents no less than that of friends has a right to be heard. Comment also is justly subject to a self-imposed restraint. It is well to be frank; it is even better to be fair. This is an ideal. Achievement in such matters is hardly given to man. We can but try, ask pardon for shortcomings, and there leave the matter.

But, granted a sufficiency of grace, to what further conquests may we look, what purpose serve, what task envisage? It is a large question, and cannot be fully answered. We are faced with a new and enormous power and a growing one. Whither is the young giant tending? What gifts does he bring? How will he exercise his privilege and powers? What influence will he exercise on the minds of men and on our public life? It cannot be pretended that an assured and entirely satisfactory answer can be given to such questions. Experience is in some respects disquieting. The development has not been all in the direction which we should most desire.

One of the virtues, perhaps almost the chief virtue, of a newspaper is its independence. Whatever its position or character, at least it should have a soul of its own. But the tendency of newspapers, as of other businesses, in these days is towards amalgamation. In proportion, as the function of a newspaper has developed and its organisation expanded, so have its costs increased. The smaller newspapers have had a hard struggle; many of them have disappeared. In their place we have great organisations controlling a whole series of publications of various kinds and even of differing or opposing politics. The process may be inevitable, but clearly there are drawbacks. As organisation grows personality may tend to disappear. It is much to control one newspaper well; it is perhaps beyond the reach of any man, or any body of men, to control half a dozen with equal success. It is possible to exaggerate the danger, for the public is not undiscerning. It recognises the authentic voices of conscience and conviction when it finds them, and it has a shrewd intuition of what to accept and what to discount.

This is a matter which in the end must settle itself, and those who cherish the older ideal of a newspaper need not be dismayed. They have only to make their papers good enough in order to win, as well as to merit, success, and the resources of a newspaper are not wholly measured in pounds, shillings, and pence. Of course the thing can only be done by competence all round, and by that spirit of co-operation right through the working staff which only a common ideal can inspire.

There are people who think you can run a newspaper about as easily as you can poke a fire, and that knowledge, training, and aptitude are superfluous endowments. There have even been experiments on this assumption, and they have not met with success. There must be competence, to start with, on the business side, just as there must be in any large undertaking, but it is a mistake to suppose that the business side of a paper should dominate, as sometimes happens, not without distressing consequences.

A newspaper, to be of value, should be a unity, and every part of it should equally understand and respond to the purposes and ideals which animate it. Between its two sides there should be a happy marriage, and editor and business manager should march hand in hand, the first, be it well understood, just an inch or two in advance. Of the staff much the same thing may be said. They should be a friendly company. They need not, of course, agree on every point, but they should share in the general purpose and inheritance. A paper is built up upon their common and successive labours, and their work should never be task work, never merely dictated. They should be like a racing boat's crew, pulling well together, each man doing his best because he likes it, and with a common and glorious goal.

That is the path of self-respect and pleasure; it is also the path of success. And what a work it is! How multiform, how responsive to every need and every incident of life! What illimitable possibilities of achievement and of excellence! People talk of "journalese" as though a journalist were of necessity a pretentious and sloppy writer; he may be, on the contrary, and very often is, one of the best in the world. At least he should not be content to be much less. And then the developments. Every year, almost every day, may see growth and fresh accomplishments, and with a paper that is really alive, it not only may, but does. Let anyone take a file of this paper, or for that matter any one of half a dozen other papers, and compare its whole make-up and leading features today with what they were five years ago, ten years ago, twenty years ago, and he will realise how large has been the growth, how considerable the achievement. And this is what makes the work of a newspaper worthy and interesting. It has so many sides, it touches life at so many points, at every one there is such possibility on improvement and excellence. To the man, whatever his place on the paper, whether on the editorial or business, or even what may be regarded as the mechanical side – this also vitally important in its place – nothing should satisfy short of the best, and the best must always seem a little ahead of the actual. It is here that ability counts and that character counts, and it is on these that a newspaper, like every great undertaking, if it is to be worthy of its power and duty, must rely.

Appendix 4

Excerpts from the 1928 Style Book
of the Manchester Guardian

NOTE.

The Authors' and Printers' Dictionary is founded on the Oxford Dictionary, and is in general agreement with the practice of the "Manchester Guardian." Below are the principal differences:—

All words ending with "ize" in both dictionaries are spelled in the "M.G." with an "s," as specialise.

Compounds are made of many words which are generally printed as one, as re-arrange, cod-fish, corn-crake, base-ball, head-quarters, life-boat, race-course, school-master. Also sergeant-major, Attorney-General, Lord-Advocate, colour-sergeant, &c. These are not to be followed.

Capital letters are sometimes oddly placed, as County palatine, County court, Monroe doctrine, Court leet. All these words should have a capital letter.

Commas and full-points are placed outside quotation marks. Only colons and semi-colons should be so placed.

Very many contractions are given, but the practice of the "M.G." is to make only usual contractions and to be sparing of them. Signatures, however, should always be followed.

5

LEADERS.

No small caps to be used. Quotation marks to be put down the side when the quoted words extend to three lines or more. Figures are not to be used below 100, except in statistics and subjects of a similar nature, also dates.

PARLIAMENTARY.

Names and titles of speakers to be in capitals, as the Marquis of SALISBURY, the CHANCELLOR of the EXCHEQUER, Mr. HODGE (Lab.—Gorton), Mr. LEACH (L.—Colne Valley), &c. Where a person is only mentioned as having spoken, the name to be in lower-case, as—"Mr. Lee also spoke." "The noble Earl," "his Lordship," the gallant Admiral, the Archbishop, the Bishop, capital letters, but "the right rev. prelate, the hon. member lower case. A capital L for the Leader of the House and the party leaders. Interjections to be printed thus:—At the end of a sentence: (Hear, hear.) (Cheers and "Hear, hear.") (Oh, oh.) (Laughter, and a Member: "Question.") No dash before these. In a sentence: —(Hear, hear)— —(cheers)— —("Oh, oh," and "Hear, hear")— —(Oh, oh)—. Act, bill, Lobby, Division Lobby, Strangers' Gallery, &c.; Front Bench (meaning the persons who sit on it), the Chair (meaning the Speaker), House, Chamber, Committee-room, Chief Whip, Whip, Clerks, Sergeant-at-Arms, the mace, bar, front bench, the chair, the throne, the woolsack, whip (a circular), first reading, second reading, third reading, committee stage, report, royal assent. Insurance Bill, Part II., section 3, subsection 1, clause 4. Estimates, Budget.

IRISH FREE STATE PARLIAMENT.

Oireachtas. Legislature: Dail Eireann, Chamber of Deputies; Seanad Eireann, Senate: Cumann na nGaedheal, Government; Clan Eireann, Constitutional Republicans; Sinn Fein, Extreme Republicans; Fianna Fail, De Valera's party.

6

LETTERS TO THE EDITOR.

Orders as to leads to be strictly followed. The contractions inst., ult., and prox. are barred—the month must be substituted. Subjoined are specimens of signatures, addresses, and dates:—

of the League of Nations would be easy.—
Yours, &c., F. LLEWELLYN-JONES.
Mold, November 12.

this difficult but most necessary and vital task.—Yours, &c.,
W. ARTHUR WESTLEY, Chairman
Oldham Branch English Church
Union.
St. John's Vicarage, Oldham,
November 17.

previous negotiations with their repre-sentatives.—Yours, &c.,
ALFRED H. COX, Medical Secretary
British Medical Association.
British Medical Association House,
Tavistock Square, London, W.C. 1,
December 9.

[As incorporation is not at present feasible, certainly it would be desirable to see what can be done by arrangement.—ED. "GUARD."] Editorial note.

The first specimen is a common form of signature. The second shows a signature in three lines, with address and date in two. The third has the signature in two lines and the address and date in three. In the first case there should be not less than four ems between &c. and the signature. Similarly, signatures to the other two should not be indented less than three and four ems to the left, all signatures being indented one em on the right, and addresses and dates one em on the left for the first line.

7

BOOK REVIEWS.

Full-headed articles take six leads, the others four. "London" before publishers' names is omitted from paragraph notices, but provincial publishers have the names of their towns prefixed, as—Derby: Bemrose and Sons. Signatures to full-headed reviews may be a separate line, but all the others must be in line with the matter where possible. Set in bourgeois. Examples:

COLLECTED POEMS. By Alfred Noyes. Vol. IV. London: Blackwood and Sons. Pp. xi. 300. 7s. 6d. net.

a day which never quite fades into the common. A. DE S.

The most obvious merit of CROMWELL, A CHARACTER STUDY, by John Drinkwater (Hodder and Stoughton, pp. 226, 2s. 6d. net). is a style which, in spite of occasional lapses,

PROPER NAMES.

Christian names should not be contracted, but contractions in signatures must be followed. Names beginning with Mac to be printed as their owners write them— MacFarlane, Macfarlane, or McFarlane. Foreign names beginning with de and von to be printed—M. de la Bere, De la Bere, Baron von der Goltz, Von der Goltz. Prefixes as follows:—M., Mme., Mlle.; Herr, Frau, Frl. (Fräulein); Señor, Señora (Spanish); Senhor, Senhora (Portuguese); Gospodin, Gospozha (Russian); Signor, Signora (Italian).

DIVISION OF WORDS.

Never divide a group of letters representing a single sound, and do not divide words at the second letter if it can be avoided. The part of the word left at the end of a line should suggest the part commencing the next line. A few words generally misdivided: Catholi-cism, fanati-cism, atmo-sphere, episco-pal, cor-re-spon-dence, archæ-ology, taut-ology, topog-raphy, prob-able. Care should be taken in dividing words, as the correcting of a wrong division entails the resetting of two lines.